ternational Airport as a purely municipal affair under a so-called 'home rule' provision of the state constitution.

For Protection

Attorney William Brinton said that in 1969, the California Supreme Court denied a hearing in a case holding that a chartered city could n o t issue revenue bonds without the majority vote (of the electorate) required under the Revenue Bond Act of 1941.

"We are filing this suit to protect San Franciscans and peninsula residents from the monumental impact of the airport expansion p l a n," said Ecology Center Director Gil Bailie.

Award

Honored

board of Stauffer Chemical Co.

He noted that he and Goldberger had just r e turned from a visit to the Denver hospital and were "tremendously impressed with the high morale of the patients and dedication of the staff."

Featured speaker at the event was Mrs. Ben K. Miller, resident member of the NJH board of trustees and life member of the hospital's women's division.

trous, outcome in the next pregnancy. Genetic counseling was indicated in these cases, he said.

It is known that the commonest result of chromosome damage is, fortunately, early miscarriage.

Chromosome Flaws

Cost Estimate

Rules in that area have yet to be determined.

Callaghan's assistant, Milton Feldstein, estimated the cost of developing measur-

TRAINING MINORITY JOURNALISTS:

A Case Study of the San Francisco Examiner Intern Program

By JUDIE TELFER

Institute of Governmental Studies

University of California, Berkeley • 1973

cided to seek policing powers over federal agencies in the state.

The State Water Resources Control Board announced yesterday it had authorized a suit against the U.S. Environmental Pollution Agency to acquire jurisdiction over federal installations discharging w a s t e water.

The federal agency gave the state authority earlier in the week to administer pollution control laws in California, except for federal agencies.

The Navy has been accused in the past of being

LOS ANGELES — University of Califo San Francisco medica ter, hit by Federal b cutbacks, is slashing growth plans nearly by Chancellor Francois S re ealed today.

The famed research training center now is ing up a new masetr for 4000 students by down from the earlier t of 7500. The reduction ply scaling down of fac students, researchers facilities a t Parn Heights.

Among the reduction a new dental schoo Fourth ave. between nassus and Kirkham nues, the subject of dr out disputes with neig hood organizations. Th ter had protested again added congestion a new structure would br the neighborhood.

Height Slashed

Sony told t h e re meeting here that his pus was now plannii structure set back fron street, which would b higher than residence the area. The struct

S. F. B. Of Pul

Though San Franci population has dropped stantially in the past decades, the number of lic servants keeps going

A study of the Departi of City Planning rele

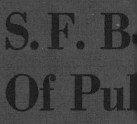

INSTITUTE OF GOVERNMENTAL STUDIES

EUGENE C. LEE, *Director*

The Institute of Governmental Studies was established in 1919 as the Bureau of Public Administration, and given its present name in 1962. One of the oldest organized research units in the University of California, the Institute conducts extensive and varied research and service programs in public policy, politics, urban-metropolitan problems and public administration.

A prime resource in these endeavors is the Institute's Library, comprising more than 333,000 documents, pamphlets and periodicals related to government and public affairs. The Library serves faculty and staff members, students, public officials and interested citizens.

In addition to its traditional Library holdings, the Institute administers the State Data Program, a teaching and research collection comprising a wide variety of machine-readable data dealing with state politics, policies and institutions. It includes public opinion polls, legislative roll calls, registration and voting statistics, characteristics of state legislatures and output measures of state policies and programs.

The Census Service Facility, administered jointly by the Institute and the Survey Research Center, makes 1970 census information available to faculty, students, local and state governments and quasi-public agencies. The facility serves as a summary tape processing center, providing computer tapes and printouts of census data, and is the prime California center for education and information concerning census material.

The Institute's professional staff is composed of faculty members who hold joint Institute and departmental appointments, research specialists, librarians and graduate students from a variety of social science disciplines. In addition, the Institute is host to visiting scholars from other parts of the United States and many foreign nations.

The Institute publishes books, monographs, periodicals, reprints, reports and bibliographies for a nationwide readership. The publications are intended to stimulate research, thought and action by scholars and public officials, with respect to significant governmental and social issues.

TRAINING MINORITY JOURNALISTS: A Case Study of the San Francisco Examiner Intern Program

TRAINING MINORITY JOURNALISTS:

A Case Study of the San Francisco Examiner Intern Program

By

JUDIE TELFER

INSTITUTE OF GOVERNMENTAL STUDIES | University of California, Berkeley
1973

Library of Congress Cataloging in Publication Data

Telfer, Judie.
    Training minority journalists.

    1. Journalism--Study and teaching--San Francisco.
2. Minorities--Education--San Francisco.
3. San Francisco Examiner. I. Title.
PN4789.C3T4   070'.07   73-4313
ISBN 0-87772-169-6

$ 4.00

Contents

Foreword

It is a truism that newspapers and other components of the mass media serve as conduits for information, but in reality the media are far more than mere pipelines. They are essential partners in a three-way relationship with government and the public, and are joined in an uneasy association marked by both mutual interdependence and a measure of mutual mistrust.

No journalist needs to be reminded that within the past few years the media have experienced new intensities of pressure and criticism from sectors of the government and the public. Some readers may not be aware, however, that media staffs are often critical of their own performance, and question the role of the mass media in a troubled society.

In San Francisco, one such effort at self-criticism produced the minority intern training program at the San Francisco *Examiner*, an ongoing project launched and conducted by staff members with the approval of the paper's publisher. *Examiner* staffers were concerned about the "shortage of minority staff members in a business that requires relevance," as well as the consequent serious lack of communication with minority groups. Thus, Lynn Ludlow, a prime mover in the *Examiner* project, expressed the hope that the minority training program would help to provide "career opportunities to persons with the ability to communicate" with those communities.

From the outset, the *Examiner's* intern program has been an honest attempt to act, "instead of just deploring." It has been imaginative and flexible, low-key and modest in scope. Some participants have called it "bumbling" and many have noted that it is understaffed. The program is also a pioneering effort in job training and placement for minority journalists. The questions it raises and its successes and failures as examined by the author are significant generally for newspaper readers and specifically for those journalists and publishers who may find the conviction to operate intern programs of their own.

Meanwhile, across the nation, only a few recent moves toward such reasonable-sounding objectives have been observed. *Help Wanted: More Black Newsmen*, a pamphlet published by the Black News Committee of APME (Associated Press Managing Editors), in a 1971 updating, listed a scant dozen of such programs nationwide. The *Examiner* program and the work of the Newsmen's Job Referral Committee (run by the same *Examiner* staff members) accounted for two out of the 12; only the Washington Journalism Center Fellowships program was older, having been established in 1965.

In the realm of argument and principle, however, a number of discussions have continued to build support for the concept of increasing the numbers and proportion of minority members on news media staffs.

It was the 1968 *Report of the National Advisory Commission on Civil Disorders* (Kerner Commission) that led the current wave of concern over press performance with respect to minorities. Chapter 15, "The Media of Mass Communications," included a section on "Reporting of Racial Problems in the United States" that was so direct and eloquent that nearly every major study of press hiring policies has mined it for quotes.

The *Columbia Journalism Review* responded in the fall of 1968 by devoting a special section to "Journalism and the Kerner Report," and has followed developments in the field of minority hiring with such stories as a report on the dwindling of minority training programs ("Side Effect," July-August 1971), and Dorothy Gilliam's article, "What Do Black Journalists Want?" (May-June 1972).

The American Newspaper Guild in *The Guild Reporter* (April 16, 1971) called on "Guild locals and members everywhere to fulfill their responsibility, first expressed by the 1947 Convention...to end minority discrimination in our industry now."

Further, Fred Taylor of *The Wall Street Journal* pointed out in the introduction of *Help Wanted*...that the booklet attempted "to inform managing editors about efforts around the country to recruit more blacks and other minorities as reporters and copy editors. That is, efforts to increase the supply--not just redistribute it through raiding." The booklet lists both special training programs and scholarships. Finally, the Petition of the Newsmen's Job Referral Committee to *Examiner* Publisher Charles Gould (May 2, 1968) (pp. 2-4) gave a clear statement of the problem and suggested a step toward its solution.

If there is substantial agreement, at least in theory, that the media should increase both the numbers and proportion of minority members on their staffs, there is somewhat less agreement on the definition of interns and what kind of training they need. The dictionary describes an intern as "an advanced student...gaining supervised practical experience..." But how advanced? How much and what kind of supervision? How much and what kind of practical experience?

Judie Telfer has indicated in her case study of the *Examiner's* intern program that a host of other questions are also still unresolved: How should interns be recruited and chosen? Does the *Examiner*-style program actually prepare interns for jobs? And above all, will interns be able to find media jobs, keep them, and advance to leadership posts? She thus presents the *Examiner* experience as a testing ground for the ideas and problems that subsequent programs must handle. A skillful reporter and interviewer, she has elicited the views and reactions of newspaper staff members, editors, publisher and interns, and to a large extent, has presented them in their own words.

Her study also permits a number of conclusions: newsmen and interns can and do learn from each other, and many find the process highly valuable. Some interns eventually get jobs, some communication with minority communities is improved, some reporters and editors gain wider perspectives. But many of the journalists affected are not decisionmakers for the industry as a whole, and they can extend their own programs only within a limited territory. Thus it seems clear that nothing less than sustained commitment and leadership at the top can move boldly enough to end the dearth of minority staff members throughout the nation's media.

The author is an experienced newspaper reporter, who began her research on this project as an undergraduate student on an honor basis in the School of Journalism at the University of California, Berkeley, in 1970. She continued the investigation through several months of 1971, and added new material in 1972. Her interest in the problem of bringing minority persons into media jobs, training and placing them, her grasp of the problems from the point of view of newspapers and interns alike, and her respect for the views of staff members and interns give her paper an immediacy and balance that should prove valuable to all those concerned with the role of newspapers in a restless and changing society.

In addition to the acknowledgements listed in the Preface, the Institute wishes to thank Judith Riggs for editorial help and Lynette Ford who was responsible for typing the monograph.

Harriet Nathan
Editor

Preface

Along with the country as a whole, the press
has too long basked in a white world, looking
out of it, if at all, with white men's eyes
and a white perspective. That is no longer
good enough. The painful process of readjust-
ment that is required of the American news
media must begin now. They must make a reality of integration--in both their product
and personnel. *(Report of the National Advisory Commission on Civil Disorders* [New York:
Bantam Books, March 1968], p.389.*)*

In response to the Kerner Report, the assassination
of Martin Luther King Jr., and the prodding of a few reporters on the staff, the San Francisco *Examiner* began
an internship program in the summer of 1968. (With
some modifications, the program is continuing in 1973.)

How was the program begun? How have interns been
recruited? What are their backgrounds? How are they
trained? How many have found jobs in the news media?
Perhaps even more important, how do they feel about the
program? And finally, how effective has the program
been?

In an attempt to answer these questions and many
others, I interviewed individuals at the *Examiner* who
have worked with the program in one capacity or another.
They included reporters Lynn Ludlow and Alan Cline
(responsible for the day-to-day workings of the program),

Publisher Charles Gould, Managing Editor Ed Dooley, City Editor Gale Cook, reporters Mary Crawford, Jim Wood and Jim Schermerhorn, and all of the first 21 interns.

I would like to thank all of the people I interviewed for allowing me to "pick their brains" and for giving me their time. The interviews were interesting and informative; they were also, without exception, extremely enjoyable. All quotations are used with the kind permission of the persons quoted.

Judie Telfer

Introduction

FROM CONFERENCE TO PROJECT

After the publication of the Kerner Report in March 1968 and the assassination of Martin Luther King Jr., in April, two San Francisco reporters determined to hold a conference to highlight the difficulty of reporting racial news. David Swanston, a white reporter for the San Francisco *Chronicle*, and his wife, Walterene Jackson Swanston, a Black reporter for the *Examiner*, were shortly to leave for jobs with the Peace Corps in Washington, D.C., and wanted to organize the conference as a last gesture or contribution to San Francisco journalism.

"I expressed the conviction that conferences were all very well but jobs were the key," said Lynn Ludlow, a white reporter at the *Examiner*. "Walterene looked me in the eye as if to say, 'Put your money where your mouth is.'" He added with a grin, "I hold her responsible for all that has happened since."

Newsmen's Job Referral Committee

As a result of Ludlow's moment of discomfiture, he, Walterene Swanston, and Alan Cline (another white *Examiner* reporter) formed the Newsmen's Job Referral Committee. Sponsors were the San Francisco Press Club, the San Francisco Human Rights Commission, the Department of Journalism at San Francisco State College

1

(later renamed California State University at San Francisco), City College of San Francisco, the San Francisco-Oakland Newspaper Guild, Sigma Delta Chi (S.F. State chapter), and Youth for Service.

The committee submitted a petition (which follows), signed by "the vast majority" of the *Examiner's* staff, proposing to the publisher, Charles A. Gould, that the paper do something about minority training. Gould responded with a letter calling for constructive proposals. The proposal for the internship program was made and approved, and the Minorities Training Program was launched.

The Petition

May 2, 1968
San Francisco, Calif.

Mr. Charles Gould,
Publisher
San Francisco *Examiner*
100 Fifth St.
San Francisco, Calif.

Dear Mr. Gould:

We solicit your support in helping create programs for getting more minority group representation on the *Examiner* staff.

As you know, President Johnson's Commission on Civil Disorders in its report issued March 1 stated "the journalistic profession has been shockingly backward in seeking out, hiring, training and promoting Negroes." The report deplored the lack of Negroes in positions of responsibility and recommended both the training and upgrading of Negro reporters.

Instead of just deploring we want to act.
And we know you do too. Guildsmen are stepping
up their activities, and we now have a committee
whose purpose is to encourage minority college
students to enter newspaper work.

We see a strong management role--in on the
job training, scholarships, grants. The paper
editorially praises such programs when developed
by other industries. We feel it is time for us
to move.

Management could finance training programs
at colleges and high schools, summer and part-
time editorial jobs, work that might stimulate
a young man or woman into coming into journalism
as a career. The paper would benefit, not only
through the talent discovered, but through the
widening links with the minority communities,
Mexican and Chinese as well as Negro.

We are not, of course, talking about tokenism,
one or two positions, but a full scale program.
We need these people. For as the President's
report states:

"If the media are to report with understanding, wisdom and sympathy on the problems of the
cities and the problems of the black man--for the
two are increasingly intertwined--they must
employ, promote and listen to Negro journalists."

We believe that comment goes for other minorities too.

Lynn Ludlow chairs a Guild minority jobs sub-
committee and can serve as a liaison to begin

discussions on machinery to get an *Examiner* program rolling.

As *Examiner* staffers we pledge our support.

cc Mr. Wells Smith
    Mr. Charles Thieriot

The Minorities Training Program

The program was planned as a series of 13-week internships, in which the interns would receive practical training in working on a newspaper. There were to be four interns in each group; later this number was reduced to two. The program was approved and recruitment started in June 1968, the same month the first group of interns started work.

A Newswriting Class

In addition to (but independent of) the Minorities Training Program, the Newsmen's Job Referral Committee organized a class in newswriting, which City College of San Francisco agreed to sponsor, and to recognize with college credit. This class met one night a week in the conference room at the *Examiner*, and was taught at various times by *Examiner* reporters Hubert Bernhard and Mary Crawford. Trainees were not required to enroll nor was the class restricted to minority members. Copy boys and interested students at C.C.S.F. have also been enrolled. The class was discontinued in 1970; it was given again in the fall sessions of 1971 and 1972 and is expected to continue in 1973.

WHO ARE THE INTERNS, AND WHAT ARE THEY DOING NOW?

By early 1971, 21 interns of minority background had completed the 13-week training program. The group

included 19 Americans, of whom 16 were Black; one was
of Filipino, one of Chinese, and one of Mexican descent.
Of the two non-Americans, one was East Indian and one
was Kenyan. At that time, nine were employed in the
news media, three were in college, one had just completed a novel, five were not employed in the news field,
and three were job-hunting. All but two had considerable college background.

The 21 interns are listed below (in alphabetical
order) with brief summaries of their backgrounds and
status as of early 1971.

Susan Almazol, 25, B.A. in sociology from the
University of California, Berkeley; was then employed
for a time as a reporter at the *Examiner*, assigned to
the Berkeley beat.

Lena Baker, 28, was graduated Phi Beta Kappa from
Drake University with a B.A. in English; worked two
years toward an M.A. at University of Iowa; was employed
as a reporter at the San Francisco *Chronicle*. Subsequently was working for an astrology magazine.

Rufus Byars, 26, "self-educated"; did not complete
high school; took some college courses; worked as a
reporter at the San Francisco *Sun-Reporter* briefly;
was doing free-lance writing. Later was editing a newspaper for Model Cities in San Francisco's Hunters Point-
Bayview district.

Trina Chope, 22, attended Radcliffe for two years;
graduated from the University of California at Berkeley
with a B.A. in social sciences; was employed briefly as
a part-time entertainment writer at the San Francisco
Chronicle. Later was attending law school in the Mid-
west.

Gail (Wells) Christian, 31, three years of college
at Pepperdine College and the University of California

at Los Angeles, majoring in history; was employed as a
legal secretary before entering the internship program;
left the program after two months to enter KQED's internship program; left KQED to enter the Columbia University
Graduate School of Journalism Summer Program, as nominee
of NBC-Los Angeles; was then working at NBC-LA.

Alonzo "Lon" Daniels, 24, B.A. in sociology at
San Francisco State College; was then employed part time
as weekend and summer relief reporter by the *Examiner*.

Louise Eubanks, 36, B.A. in journalism from San
Francisco State College; had completed her first novel
and was waiting to hear from the publisher. During
1972 was editing *In Title One*, a newspaper issued by
the Berkeley Unified School District.

Lance Gilmer, 29, B.A. in American Civil War history at Roosevelt University in Chicago; worked as
a teacher, community organizer, and photographer in
Chicago before entering the program; was then employed
as a sports reporter at the *Examiner*.

Cherise Green, 24, attended Holy Names College,
University of California, Berkeley, and San Francisco
State College. Worked briefly at the Oakland *Post*; was
not then employed.

Gregory Gross, 19, journalism major at California
State College at Hayward; worked as a summer replacement reporter at the *Examiner* during the summer of 1970;
then was working for Associated Press in San Francisco,
also in the summer.

Richard Harris, 24, B.A. in journalism from
Sacramento State College; was hired as a reporter at
the Sacramento *Bee*; went on leave for four months for
a fellowship at the Washington Journalism Center; then

returned to work at the *Bee*. In 1972 was on the staff
of Berkeley Assemblyman John J. Miller.

Christopher Kabungura, 31, B.A. in journalism from
California State College at Hayward; was then seeking
a job in the news media; meanwhile, was teaching Swahili
part time at City College of San Francisco.

Christopher Knowles, 34, attended school through
the eleventh grade; completed high school through exam-
ination while in the service; was then employed as a
photographer at the San Jose *Mercury-News*.

Jim Lee, 31, B.A. in sociology from the University
of Oregon; began work toward M.A. in sociology at San
Francisco State College; sold real estate; was employed
as a sports reporter at the Las Vegas *Review-Journal*,
and then was working in public relations in Las Vegas.

Jim Logan, 21, attended Diablo Valley College;
then enrolled at Stanislaus State College in Turlock;
a senior in sociology.

Leslie McBee, 23, B.A. in psychology from the
University of San Francisco; was then seeking a job in
the news media.

Kieran Manjarrez, 23, B.A. (no major) at St. John's
College in Santa Fe, New Mexico; was seeking a job in
the news media. Later was studying law at Hastings
College of the Law in San Francisco.

Jehangir Patel, 25, attended one year of college
in Bombay, India; B.A. in political science at Yale
University; was later employed as labor reporter at the
Hartford (Connecticut) *Times*. Had returned to Bombay,
but expected to come back to the U.S. to seek another
newspaper job.

David Randolph, 23, studied law enforcement for a year and a half at Merritt College, Oakland; was then employed as a photographer at the San Francisco *Chronicle*.

Orville Springs, 29, attended the University of Colorado for four years (no degree), majoring in international relations; was employed for two years as a sales agent by Pan American Airlines before entering the internship program; was hired as a reporter by the *Examiner* and sponsored by the *Examiner* for the Columbia University Graduate School of Journalism Summer Program; dropped out of the program and gave up his job at the *Examiner*; was not then seeking employment in the news media.

Hollis Wagstaff, 21, was attending Contra Costa College and planned to enroll at San Francisco State in the fall of 1971, majoring in journalism; was employed as a copy boy at the *Examiner* and later became a night reporter there.

Some Later Arrivals

By the summer of 1972, the *Examiner* program had added two interns in the regular series and had begun a summertime session. The regulars were Shih-Shung Quon, who spent some time at the Journalism Center, Washington, D.C. and was currently working on a Master's degree at Columbia University; and Michael G. Looney, who left a job as copy boy at the Oakland *Tribune*, returned to the *Tribune* and became a reporter.

The three-month summertime session in 1972 brought in Gloria Carillo and Charleta Johnson as reporter trainees and Marilynn K. Yee as a photo trainee. Gloria Carillo had worked as a legal secretary and had finished her sophomore year at the University of California, Berkeley; Charleta Johnson is in her senior year at Berkeley. Marilynn Yee is studying photo-journalism at California State University at San Jose.

For the winter of '72-73, plans called for two interns who would participate in six-month sessions.

A CURRENT LOOK AT SELECTED BAY AREA NEWSPAPERS

Definitions of "intern" and "training" programs vary considerably. By late 1972, none of the papers queried reported intern projects along the lines of the *Examiner's* program. The Berkeley *Gazette* and Richmond *Independent* had no such program; the San Jose *Mercury* provided no special training but indicated equal opportunity hiring.

The Palo Alto *Times* (as of January 1973) has had minority training programs "dating back almost 10 years," but ended experimental programs about two years ago. The *Times* has a cooperative arrangement with California State University at San Jose for intern training that is "not limited solely to minorities."

The San Francisco *Chronicle* had embarked on a "learn-by-doing" program hiring people without experience, at starting reporter's scale. Three members of the *Chronicle* program included Don Lau (photographer), Karen Howze (reporter), and Boku Kodama (copy desk). All had college background: Don Lau studied at and Boku Kodama graduated from California State University at San Francisco; and Karen Howze is a graduate of the University of Southern California.

II

Formulating the Program

The organizers took an empirical approach in assembling the three main elements in the training program: the interns to be recruited, the teachers who were to instruct and supervise, and the body of knowledge and experience to be gained. In their petition to Publisher Charles Gould, the Newsmen's Job Referral Committee had indicated that their purpose was "to encourage minority college students to enter newspaper work." Thus local college campuses could be expected to provide some recruits, but other sources were not foreclosed. *Examiner* reporters were to comprise the faculty, with varying degrees of teaching experience, while the laboratory was to be the city and the newspaper itself.

RECRUITMENT: APPROACHES AND PROBLEMS

Recruiting methods have varied almost as much as the interns themselves. For the most part, the *Examiner* put out feelers and then waited for applicants to come forward. Recruitment was mostly by word of mouth. Lynn Ludlow, for example, spoke to college groups and phoned journalism departments, the Economic Opportunity Council, and Youth for Service.

The writer asked each of the 21 interns interviewed in this study how he or she learned of the

program. Nine reported hearing of it from teachers or
others at college; five heard from *Examiner* employees;
one received a call from Lynn Ludlow, who was teaching
at San Francisco State, where she was a student. The
other six learned about the program from friends.

When the applicant inquired about the program at
the *Examiner*, he was asked to submit either samples of
writing or an essay stating his reasons for wanting
to work for a newspaper.

According to City Editor Gale Cook, the *Examiner*
was not "what you would call swamped with applicants,
which was just as well. We've had about twice as many
as we could accept." Ludlow said he tried hard not to
over-recruit because "I dislike saying no--you recruit
five and you have two spots. That's terrible, especially when you have no alternatives to offer."

Nevertheless, he called the recruiting arm of the
program "inadequate." "The first group was all college
students," he said, "representing all the Black journalism students in the Bay Area--four." He attributed the
difficulty in recruiting to several causes: In the high
schools, "If students aren't getting a B average or better, or if they get a C in English, they can't work for
the high school newspaper. The upshot of this is that
even when a school is 80 percent Black and 20 percent
white, the school paper is something like 80 percent
white and 20 percent Black. The idiot counselors don't
realize that if a person likes working on a school paper
his English grades will improve."

The lack of models to emulate is another factor,
Ludlow believed. "Having more Black television reporters
helps, but a newspaper byline is impersonal. You can't
tell by a name whether a reporter is Black or white or
what, so it's no model." Finally, "Some say no self-
respecting Black person would work for the Hearst
Examiner. There may be something to that, but...[that

attitude] hasn't occurred among any of the initial contacts yet. At any rate, it's not something measurable."

Staff Views on Qualifications

Another problem in recruiting was to determine
qualifications. What degree of education should be
required? Initially, the *Examiner* had hoped to reach
hard-core unemployed men and women who otherwise would
not have a chance for a break of any kind. Jim Wood,
the *Examiner* education writer, felt this was wrong:

> The program is so small that it's not going to
> have any serious impact on employment or on the
> so-called hard-core unemployed. But a program
> of this size *can* make real impact on another
> serious problem and that is the lack of minority
> group members in the working press. I don't
> think it should be just a gig; I think it should
> be a training program for people who are in-
> terested in getting into the news business. I
> think there's a really serious need right now
> to bring more minority group members into the
> business.

Both Mary Crawford (who taught the evening class
in newswriting) and Alan Cline commented on the difficulties of teaching basic writing skills within a
limited time span. The 13-week program, Cline said,
"is only long enough for someone with a college background who has done considerable writing. You can't
help the hard core until you have someone who can give
full time to supervision of the program, and even then
it would take at least a year. There are certain things
that you have to have on a newspaper. You have to be
able to write a declarative sentence; you have to be
able to express yourself. I think these things can be
learned, but I think it takes an awful lot of time."

Mary Crawford agreed that grammar cannot be taught in one semester,but if the students come armed with a knowledge of basic English, "they can learn the basic techniques of newswriting, reporting and research; how to use the city directory, government directories--you have to be a pretty good cop as well as writer. These things, basic news techniques for television, radio, and newspaper, can be taught in one semester."

On the basis of experience with several "intern classes," Ludlow asserted, "A commitment to a journalism career is now a prerequisite for the program." Wood agreed: "I think in recruiting there should be an effort to get interns who are likely to go into the news business and who have a good chance of succeeding."

Mary Crawford emphasized the point that the evening class, in particular, provided an excellent opportunity to judge an applicant's interest in communications. "If they don't want to go into communications, they probably still have learned something very valuable. I think a good way to find out about whether you want to be in the business or not is to take one of these courses or get into the intern program--find out young."

The *Examiner* had originally hoped to reach people who were underemployed and those from other fields who might be interested in a different career. According to Cline, "The program simply didn't work out that way. Obviously people don't like to give up good jobs. It practically gave Orville [Springs] an ulcer. He was on his way to a career. To give that up for the insecurity of the program was giving up a hell of a lot."

Some Lessons from the Washington *Star*

The Washington (D.C.) *Star* instituted a minority training program with results that may suggest answers to some of the problems faced by the *Examiner*. The *Star's* program apparently was also instigated by Walterene Swanston, when she worked there.

The *Star* chose three minority persons from "target areas" or disadvantaged neighborhoods, offered them a year's training, provided extra schooling where necessary, and guaranteed them jobs after successful completion of the training. Warren Howard of the *Star* discussed the program with Ludlow, and foresaw its future as shaky. Two of the three trainees have already been let go by the *Star*, in the belief they would not succeed in the news business. Apparently one defect of the program lay in the initial selection of trainees.

TRAINING AND SUPERVISION

Training: The Art of Writing

At the *Examiner*, a flexible pattern was followed in training. During the first week or two of each program, interns prepared rewrites and obituaries, reworking the material until it satisfied the supervisor. Next, they took part in what City Editor Gale Cook called "parallel reporting"; that is, they followed a reporter on his story, then returned to the office to write their own versions. Eventually they were sent out on beats (prescribed rounds that cover specific areas of interest, as the city hall beat) or assigned to cover news or feature stories by themselves.

Interns' stories were analyzed by Alan Cline or Lynn Ludlow. Ludlow described his method of analyzing a story in this way: "I start with the format--see if it's got the slug [identification] in the right place. Then I talk about the style-book style. Then I talk about the writing: make the sentences shorter, use more effective verbs. Then I talk about it as a news story, given that lead. Finally I talk about the lead. I take about half an hour for one page of copy, but I think it pays off."

Every story written by an intern had some chance of getting into the paper, according to Ludlow. "Writing for publication makes people far more receptive to learning their lessons. The importance of spelling someone's name right doesn't really hit you until it might get into the paper." Sixteen of the 21 interns interviewed had stories published with bylines; at least 18 of the 21 reported that some of their stories were published.

Most interns spent some time on beats, particularly city hall and police, usually a week on each. Several interns worked in special departments. For example, Richard Harris spent a week each in the women's and television departments; Christopher Knowles worked only in the sports department and in the city room; Jim Lee worked a few weeks in the sports department and Lance Gilmer only in sports.

Interns who made a special effort to broaden their experience were given a variety of assignments. Louise Eubanks, for example, "did about everything there was to do on that *Examiner*. I guess they still remember me as one who got around; everything is fascinating to me. I just went around and introduced myself and asked questions." Gregory Gross did just about everything a reporter can possibly do in 13 weeks:

> Most of my work was in the city room, but I spent
> a week with the police beat and a week with the
> federal court beat. I even did a little unoffi-
> cially as a photographer, mainly because of my
> very strong interest. I spent a week riding with
> a unit of the Oakland Police Department from
> 4 p.m. to midnight. This was not an assignment;
> I asked to do it. I wrote a story based on the
> things I saw and heard in eight hours, and they
> ran it with a byline.

Both Cline and reporter Jim Schermerhorn emphasized the importance of training in rewrite. Cline said, "Rewrites are necessary. You have got to be able to write a sentence and think in terms of how a story is put together. This is the key tool. It isn't just running out and getting the big story."

Schermerhorn bestowed almost poetic significance on the rewrite:

...young people generally have little patience with writing two-paragraph handouts and obits. The pro thinks this is part of the craft and deserves as much attention as the front-page late-breaking news story. It's difficult to explain why this is so important. Most of them little by little begin to sense this: Each task, no matter how small, is a challenge to his craftsmanship and he can take some joy in it.

It's fun to hand a six-page handout by some publicity sharp to a youngster with a note: "Two paragraphs." There's great joy in watching a face light up if they find the meat in the story and bring up something that's clean and crisp and lovely. Then you know here is a person who can do a complex series, in time. Then you know you have got a newspaperman.

Managing Editor Ed Dooley would have liked to see more trainees spend time on the copy desk: "I've thought about that for our own staff, too. I spent 10 years on the Denver *Post* and they set up one spot on the copy desk for a reporter--out of it we found good ones."

Intern Lance Gilmer thought he had too much of a good thing. "I did 'shorts' (little four or five paragraph stories) all day long. I think it's nice when you start off, but after a while doing shorts gets to you. The first week was very exciting--the second week I got a little tired of it--by the 18th week, I was really up-tight." He became a sports reporter on the *Examiner*, "but I got to be well known for writing shorts and they expect me still to do it."

The second group of interns was asked to write "specials" or "term papers." Ludlow called it "not a bad idea." It gives them experience, he said, "in putting together a long project, teaches them a bit of investigation, and gives them a good story with a byline to put in their portfolio."

Staffing and Supervision: How Much and What Kind?

The amount of supervision varied with the apparent needs of the trainee and other demands on the *Examiner* staff. In general, supervision or advice was available if requested. Lance Gilmer complained that he had very little supervision: One reason was that Ludlow was in New York during most of Gilmer's time in the program. Gregory Gross, who had considerable freedom, appreciated the implied compliment, but compared the experience of being sent alone on an assignment to being "tossed into the Mekong Delta with a slingshot."

The burden of supervision fell most heavily on Ludlow and was in addition to his regular job. Ludlow himself said, "The committee [Newsman's Job Referral Committee] is supposed to recruit and do placement. The *Examiner* tries to release them for supervision. What is really required, of course, is somebody who would be detailed on a regular basis to look out for the needs of the trainees."

Schermerhorn added, "A lot of the interns feel there should be more formalized direction of the program. A lot of them feel they wasted some time just sitting around the office. I think that's true. It's a problem that's common in the newspaper business with people breaking in. This wasn't an intern problem specifically, but rather it was a problem of people who are entering the newspaper business whether they are in an intern program or just starting out as reporters. It was true when I was breaking in and I think it's true with anyone."

Ludlow pointed out a problem area related to supervision: "The *Examiner* is a soft-sell, no-directive type of city room. They really let you do your own thing. If you look busy, it's okay. This suits people who are self-starters, but many of the trainees think this is the way it is. They're in for a horrible shock when they go to work for another paper. Many of them have adopted our worst habits: arrive late, take a long lunch and take off early. They require supervision."

After the initial three groups of four interns each had completed their training, the program was cut back to admit only two interns at a time. Ludlow explained that this move was made so that the staff could supervise the interns more closely. The cutback took effect immediately after Rufus Byars's group had finished training. Byars had blasted the program in an article in the Black newsmen's *Ball & Chain Review* (pp.33-36). Moreover Byars considered the timing more than coincidental: "They never want another Rufus because Rufus was hard core. I think they could supervise two. They could supervise as many as they wanted to train. It's no problem having a shadow; all you need to do is get extra seats."

Extensions of the Training Period

Beginning with the second group of trainees, nearly every 13-week appointment was extended for an additional four weeks or longer. During the extensions, the pay was set at scale for beginning reporters. The extensions gave the trainee additional experience and the *Examiner* a chance to scrutinize, under more authentic conditions, a potential *Examiner* employee.

Some trainees on extension, however, felt they had been kept dangling longer than necessary, and that extensions only served to prolong their uncertainty about employment.

ESTIMATING COSTS

Interns were paid at the rate designated in the San Francisco-Oakland Newspaper Guild contract for "copy boy with less than three months of experience." As of early 1971 (based on the contract signed in December 1970) the pay was $95 a week. Before the new contract, the pay had been $84 a week, and at the beginning of the program, in 1968, it was $75 a week.

The total cost of the program to the *Examiner* would of course include more than simply the interns' pay, and therefore is difficult to calculate. Ludlow thought that at least one-half of his and perhaps one-quarter of Cline's effectiveness as a reporter was lost to the paper because of time spent with the interns. Other members of the *Examiner* staff spent smaller fractions of their time on the program.

Using $85 per week as an average for intern pay, the cost of the program was $23,205 for 21 interns, or about $1,100 per intern, exclusive of staff costs. Extra desks and equipment were not required; interns were assigned to desks normally occupied by reporters on another shift. Salaries paid to interns whose appointments were extended cannot properly be included in an estimate of program costs because during the extensions the interns were functioning as cub reporters and producing stories for the paper. Thus the interns' pay plus the value of the staff time spent with them were the basic costs to be considered.

As Ludlow pointed out, "The cost has to be as low as any professional training program in the country. Columbia has a 10-week summer program (for 36 students), half television and half print, and sponsored by the Ford Foundation. The cost is $350,000 for the summer." This would amount to nearly $10,000 per student.

Charles Gould, publisher of the *Examiner*, when asked
if he felt that the cost of the program was burdensome,
claimed that the cost had never been calculated before
and that no one had previously asked the question. As
to whether the *Examiner* was getting its money's worth
out of the interns, Gould said:

> I don't think we should ever put the program on
> a dollars-and-cents basis. I couldn't say that
> we are getting our money's worth out of any sin-
> gle individual on the staff. The overall mix is
> something that satisfies the editors and the
> end product satisfies our readers. I would be
> quite unhappy if we ever got down to the point of
> trying to measure the individual contributions
> of the interns or working reporters on a day-to-
> day basis. In fact, I'd hate to have such a
> yardstick used on my own endeavors.

THE EMPLOYMENT RECORD

The employment record of the program stands as follows: As of early 1971, two-thirds, or 14 of the 21,
had found jobs in the news media; five had left those
jobs for various reasons, and nine (about 40 percent)
remained employed. Of the nine interns who were employed in early 1971, all but two reported that the
Newsmen's Job Referral Committee had helped them. (Those
hired by the *Examiner* are included in this "helped"
category.)

The two exceptions were Dave Randolph and Gail
Christian. Randolph found no openings at the end of
his training period. He returned to school, then heard
about a job as a summer replacement at the *Chronicle*,
and was hired as a permanent staff member at the end
of the summer. Gail Christian left the *Examiner* program
to enter KQED's training program and subsequently left

that program to be sponsored for the Columbia University Graduate School of Journalism by NBC-Los Angeles.

Six trainees were hired by the *Examiner*: Susan Almazol, Lena Baker, Trina Chope, Lon Daniels, Lance Gilmer and Orville Springs. Orville Springs dropped out of the summer program at Columbia, for which the *Examiner* was sponsoring him, and thus forfeited his job at the paper. Lena Baker and Trina Chope left permanent positions at the *Examiner* to take jobs at the *Chronicle*.

Jim Lee reported that the interns were given complete access to the telephones and were allowed to make long distance calls at the *Examiner's* expense in their quest for jobs. He answered an ad in *Editor and Publisher* magazine from the Las Vegas *Review-Journal*, and found that, "since the whole thing [the intern program] is so rare, most small town dailies will be very impressed with it. They would have hired me over the phone, but had to have me out for an interview to make it look good. It turned out the he [the editor of the Las Vegas paper] was trying to sell the job to me."

Even Rufus Byars, the program's most vociferous critic, admitted that it was because of the *Examiner* program that the *Sun-Reporter* hired him. "I had applied at the *Sun-Reporter* nine months before the program and they wouldn't hire me then because I didn't have a name. It helped me get in, if that was what I wanted." He said that the committee lined up interviews for him and provided recommendations. "They really wanted to get rid of me--wanted to find a place for me." And most of the interns who were still in school expressed confidence that the *Examiner* and the Newsmen's Job Referral Committee would assist them and give them good recommendations when they did seek a job.

Although only three of the interns have left the San Francisco Bay Area for jobs, smaller towns still seem to present the most fertile opportunities, just as they do for inexperienced white reporters, and the trainees who have taken jobs outside the Bay Area had no difficulty in securing employment.

Jim Schermerhorn said of the interns, "I think many of them--most of them--would be extremely valuable on a small newspaper in a small community. It's tough to explain to them how much joy there is in practicing your craft on a newspaper which has, say, a circulation of 50,000 in the county, and where you learn the obligation to spell a name right in an obituary and feel the need to be almost inhumanly accurate and kind and humane. I think you lose a lot of that on a big paper, where there's less personal hurt in making an error. The attitude [in a big town] is pretty much, 'We'll wait and hear from a lawyer.' You know if you hurt someone like a mayor, he always has access to the courts and so you don't feel so bad about it. But other people are not so able to take care of themselves.

"The *Examiner* is generally gracious enough to be ashamed *after* making an error that damages somebody. Some aren't.

"Also in a smaller community you know how police work. You watch the drunks and prostitutes and people in trouble. You learn law and something of the actions of the lower courts. We never see them here. We get a story off the radio and follow up by phone." He added his view that "The practical thing to do right now is to hie out for the country's better newspapers--the Denver *Post*, Washington *Post*, etc., because minority people *are* constantly in demand."

III
Interns' Reactions to the Program

How did the interns themselves judge the program? Their evaluations and responses emerged in at least three forms: (1) answers to open-ended interview questions; (2) written memos, notes and articles; and (3) reactions to the written commentaries, including views expressed by both interns and staff members.

SOME PERSONAL EVALUATIONS

Interns generally have felt that their 13 or more weeks in the *Examiner* training program were personally worthwhile, as they indicated in their evaluations during the course of the interviews. A selection of their responses is given here, with additional comments in the excerpted transcripts of the interviews, beginning on page 66.

All but one of the interns now working on a newspaper agreed that the *Examiner* gave them at least a sound basis for their current jobs. The exception was Lance Gilmer, *Examiner* sports reporter, who gave the program a "poor" rating. "I wasn't trained," he said. "The only reason I'm sitting in this room right now is because I'm Black. I don't even know if I'm qualified."

Rufus Byars, who worked briefly on the *Sun-Reporter*, maintained that he "didn't get anything out of the *Examiner* program except hypocrisy....What I really needed at the *Examiner* I didn't get until I got to the *Sun-Reporter*--word usage and the five *w*'s (the who, what, when, where, why information)....The *Examiner* program is tediously slow for anyone who knows what he's after."

Jehangir Patel had many specific criticisms, but he described the program emphatically as "excellent" and "outstanding," and seemed to bubble over with enthusiasm for it. He emphasized that his criticisms were made not to try to debunk the program, but to help make it more meaningful.

Susan Almazol said, "It really helped me, but I had a B.A. and was a pretty good writer to begin with....It's a really good program for some people, not for others. It doesn't teach you how to write; it teaches you newspaper techniques."

Richard Harris commented, "I think it's a really good program...helpful...to the mass media. You can't just go in there and expect to let them pour it into your head. You've got to dig. I have a lot more to learn, too."

"Interesting, for one," said Hollis Wagstaff, in evaluating the program. "We would run a lot and had to deal with different human beings and different situations. I like it because it taught me quite a few things--taught me how to deal with people."

"The ultimate goal is to get you employed," said Lon Daniels, "to get you working at a paper. At least this is Lynn's goal. But I think the program offers so much more than that. You can learn about the city, how it functions, the courts--a lot of things that I maybe should have learned in college. It's almost like doing field work for the classes that you took in college."

"I would give it an S," said Cherise Green. "I think they are still experimenting....I don't even know what to tell them to do but play it by ear and do like they have been doing. They're trying to do something, that's obvious, and it's not like they're trying to save face. And it really helps. What it does is just turn people onto something and give them an opportunity."

In Jim Logan's view, "It definitely was a good program. It exposed me to a lot of things I would never have seen otherwise, and I met a lot of people I wouldn't have met. Maybe it helped the *Examiner* as far as public relations went. When I introduced myself as an *Examiner* trainee, people felt the *Examiner* was doing something. But I felt this program was a sincere effort on the *Examiner's* part to encourage Black people to go into journalism."

Louise Eubanks said: "There were aspects of the program that were frustrating, but I have never met a reporter that wasn't frustrated. It's just plain frustrating, the whole job, so there's nothing new or uncommon in my being frustrated. The rules don't come from the reporters but from higher up. I think I would have had more difficulty in getting a job without the program because papers respect it. It's far more valuable that just a B.A. in journalism; it talks a lot louder. I have a greater chance now to get a job than my white counterpart."

NOTE BY GREGORY GROSS

Gregory Gross expressed his feelings publicly in a glowing thank you note, which he pinned on the *Examiner* bulletin board on his last day in the program.

ETERNAL THANKS

The common cry of all young men everywhere is "just give me a break--just one chance!"

All too many of those young men are old men by
the time they get the break. Some never get it.

That's why, if I stand out at all from the rest
of the desperate young men, it is because I got
my chance, I got the break.

YOU gave it to me.

You took me in, helped me where I needed help,
encouraged me when I needed encouragement, ad-
vised in the way a reporter should go.

In all, you gave me a four-year education in
three brief--too brief--months.

All I could do in return was work here, and
that's not even a minimal payment.

When I return to school, my fellow journalism
students will ask me what it's like to work for
a big metropolitan newspaper.

I will tell them how it feels to work with a
magnificent collection of beautiful human beings.

Eternal thanks.

                              Gregory Alan Gross

INTERNS' MEMO OF EVALUATION FROM TRINA AND SUSAN

        Trina Chope and Susan Almazol presented a written
evaluation of the program for City Editor Gale Cook.
The memo and Ludlow's comments are presented below because they deal with many of the questions and problems
raised by the interns.

memo to gale cook

from: trina and susan

re: minority training program

MAIN CRITICISMS:

1. need more time to learn journalism tech-
    niques before covering stories.
2. lack of supervision.
3. too unstructured; often, nothing to do.
4. 13 weeks--too short a training period.

SUGGESTED SOLUTIONS:

1. first 2 weeks should be spent in city room
    to learn rules of game (e.g. 'more than'
    rather than 'over').
    -practice writing with obits and handouts.
    -one day during 1st week should be spent on
     all day tour of the plant to learn how news-
     paper is put together.
    -two days (one per week) should be spent fol-
     lowing reporters around to get a feeling for
     what should be reported and how. intern
     should not be responsible for writing a
     story.

2. 3rd to about 8th week should be spent cov-
    ering and writing stories.
    -a reporter should be responsible for spe-
     cific intern for one whole day.
    -this reporter would be responsible for:
     matching interns with reporters on stories;
     critiquing stories;
     acting as liaison between city desk and
     intern (e.g. who is to write story to be
     published).

3. there should be a weekly evaluation session
   with interns, lynn, alan and other reporters
   who worked with interns that week. we think
   gale should sit in on sessions occasionally.
   -let interns know how they are progressing.
   -point out interns' weaknesses (in writing
    ability only!)
   -air interns' gripes (for regular feedback).
   -perhaps, talk about current job possibil-
    ities to facilitate interns' own placement
    efforts later.

4. 8th to 11th weeks should be spent outside
   city room.
   -federal beat
   -city hall beat
   -sunday section
   -sports or women's
   -one day each at copy and news desks (because
    we're not clear on what they're supposed to
    be doing).

5. 12th and 13th weeks should be spent in city
   room with emphasis on individual initiative
   and on placement.

6. OPTION TO BE EXPLORED EARLY IN PROGRAM WITH
   INTERN: TERM PROJECT
   we have mixed feelings about this. we hated
   doing one, but susan thinks she really learned
   a lot about researching a story, interviewing
   and finding out about one's subject. perhaps,
   if the project is carefully limited and supervised, it could be a really good learning and
   fun experience.

We feel that the philosophy of the training program should be spelled out and made clear to
everyone involved.

Is the program to serve the newspaper business
or minority communities?

Is the program seeking minority spokesmen or simply minority faces in city room?

Is the program to recruit and train hard-core ghetto types for the mass media or simply to give experience to any minority person?

Is the program seeking the perspectives of minority reporters or simply recruiting reporters with "entrance privileges" on certain stories?

When these questions are settled, perhaps interns will no longer worry about their obligations (if any) to the program and reporters won't feel they have been "kicked in the ass" when the program is criticized.

ADDITIONAL SUGGESTIONS:

susan thinks the number of interns should be limited to 2 because two can be easily supervised. she also thinks they should be hired as "editorial assistants" with $121/week salary because it's really, really difficult to live on the $62 weekly she received as a trainee.

trina thinks four interns should be trained at a time because as many people as can be handled should be trained, and four have been trained in a session before.

LYNN LUDLOW'S COMMENTS ON THE MEMO

Lynn Ludlow's personal, written reactions to Trina Chope's and Susan Almazol's criticism:

Let's discuss the minority memo page by page.

The first page offers practical, intelligent and simple solutions to various problems.

It could most easily be applied if you could
give the trainee supervisor a full half day,
perhaps Thursday afternoons, to do two things:
1. Set up the weekly evaluation session.
2. Plan for the following week's trainee
    activities. This means drawing up a sched-
    ule, briefing the staffers involved,
    etc., or discussing individual problems.

This will not work unless the supervisor is kept
free of daily news stories, including those he
may have initiated himself. The person acting
as supervisor can change from week to week, if
necessary. Besides myself and Al, supervisors
could include Wood, Belcher, Dum, Cone, Melnick.

The philosophy angle is important to Susan and
Trina--as for myself, I think it's better to
just figure vaguely that somehow the program is
a good kind of idea and let everyone involved
think up whatever philosophy he prefers.

However, these are my views as reflected in the
original intern proposal and in subsequent writings or discussions.
1. Does the program serve the newspaper busi-
    ness or the minority communities?
It serves both, of course. The minority communities are presumably to be served with more effective and more sensitive news coverage. However,
I feel strongly that any program set up *primarily*
or *exclusively* for minority communities should
be sponsored, planned and administered by those
communities. If pressed, I believe this program
is *primarily* aimed at serving the communications
media--in particular, the large, metropolitan,
general circulation daily newspaper, and, in general, the public served by this newspaper. Unless

the newspapers can somehow better serve their
own urban communities, they will continue to fade
from the scene. To the extent that newspapers
serve the urban community in general, they also
serve the various minority groups that compose
the urban community.

2. Is the program seeking minority spoksmen or
   simply minority faces in the city room?

Neither. The program seeks persons with the
special ability to communicate with minority
communities. The minority communities have many
spokesmen, but few reporters with this ability
to interpret or convey accurately the views
of those who are spokesmen. As for "minority
faces in the newsroom," this suggests the worst
form of tokenism--the person hired for a job he
cannot handle or is not permitted to handle.
We are definitely not interested in a tokenism
program that has the inevitable effect of dam-
aging the "minority faces" and the effectiveness of the newspaper itself.

3. Is the program to recruit and train hard-
   core ghetto types for the mass media or simply to give experience to any minority person?

Neither. As stated above, the program is intended to provide career opportunities to persons
with the ability to communicate with minority
communities. The *Examiner* and the Printco
should probably institute programs intended to
provide careers to the hard-core ghetto persons,
but this is not such a program. It would be
presumptuous for us to differentiate somehow
between a hard-core ghetto type person and "any
minority person"--presumably, a person from a
minority background who has lost his credentials
as a minority spokesman because of some presumed
economic or educational advantage.

4. Is the program seeking the perspectives
   of minority reporters or simply recruiting
   reporters with "entrance privileges" on
   certain stories?

Both. And more, besides. U.S. society is changing, fragmenting into groups. At one time, newspapers could perceive a certain fundamental set of assumptions that would offer a platform for objectivity, interpretation and impartiality. This is less true now. Consequently, newspapers should seek reporters with the ability to communicate with those groups which do not share this platform of basic assumptions. The reasons for this theory are based on what I know of contemporary research and speculation into communication theory as well as dabblings into McLuhan, contemporary sociology and the like. But as I said above, it's a lot easier to say the intern program is "a good idea" and avoid hangups on ideology.

One additional note: As each intern learns more of the role of the newspaper reporter and begins to explore his own career possibilities, he may wish to specialize in the reporting of news from minority communities (like Rush Greenlee) or he may prefer to handle general news or whatever. I think it best that we offer this option to interns and not impose from above our own notions on what is best for them.

I doubt very much if the settlement of these questions will end misunderstandings, personality problems and individual difficulties on the part of interns, staffers or outsiders. I suppose it's a problem worth considering, but I doubt very much that philosophy will solve the overall problem of the shortage of minority persons in a business that requires relevance.

                                        Lynn

RUFUS BYARS'S ARTICLE

The most outspoken critic of the *Examiner's* minority training program was Rufus Byars, who blasted the program in an article, "Training or Indoctrination?" which appeared in the October 1969 issue of *Ball & Chain Review*, a newspaper published by Bay Area Black journalists. The article is included here in full with the permission of *Ball & Chain Review*.

"The black man is making progress today," proclaims Mighty Whitey. "He's into more of the mainstream than he has ever been in his history," they further elaborate. "It's never been a matter of not wanting black people in good working positions. It always appeared as though they (those strange contradictions of mankind--Black People) just never were able to adjust to the complicated struggles of competitive survival."

It was this sort of encouragement that forced me to probe my stability, that demanded of me recognition of my humanity, and forced me to find out why I had been labeled as three-fourths beast and one-fourth human (meaning that I did possess a few human characteristics).

Late one evening, about nine months ago, I received a phone call, from a social service affiliate of mine. He informed me of a training program that was going into effect at the San Francisco *Examiner*.

"Well Rufus," he said, "it's not a sure thing, but it has its compensations. It will give you more of the writing experience you need, and maybe, just maybe, it will open the door to the news media for you."

Excited, that wasn't the half of it, I was literally thrilled to death. Here I was, Rufus, a

black who had been writing for the past six and
a half years receiving merely rebuffs from my
kind concerning my strong desire to tell it like
it is.

After contacting Lynn Ludlow, head of the training program, I was told to bring excerpts of my.
previous writings with me when I came for my
interview. At this time in my writing career,
I had been working on a psychological-philosophical
work called "Lifeline."

Although the essays called for someone with deep
insights, insofar as understanding them was concerned, I stood totally assured that here [meaning
at the *Examiner*] my work would be truly acknowledged and appreciated for its valuable content.

Unfortunately I didn't look before I leaped and
the disappointment nearly shattered my conception
of what the intellectual man was supposed to
be. I was continuously informed of how not to
write in my previous fashion and that the news
form was the most acceptable to the reading
public. Therefore I adjusted.

Yet there was something about this training program that rubbed me the wrong way. I found many
of the working personnel more concerned with my
ideological convictions, than with making me a
good writer. The program was to reach into the
hard-core ghetto areas and pick out those minorities who showed promise. I showed promise. However, there was yet another reason--a reason
other than making me a good newsman--involved in
this training program. I was to be remolded, re-
programmed on what were the essential values in
life.

More time was spent debating my mental frame of
mind than anything else. I found during this program, that the white man can't merely train a black

for a specific profession, he's got to remake
this black: Reconstruct into his being a white
outlook on things and situations. I went into
the program with the idea of opening communi-
cative doorways between two totally alienated
peoples. Yet I found this not to be the function
of the white press.

Many times I observed the demoralization of Rush
Greenlee, another black on the *Examiner* staff.
They would send the man out to cover a story--
and you can believe that nine and a half times out
of ten it was a colored story--then debate with
him on whether he heard what he said he heard,
or saw what he thought he saw.

To me this was an education in the underhanded
workmanship of the "Good Doing" white race.
There before me, each day, sat an example of what
I would be if I allowed myself to be rewired by
this lousy electrician.

There is a sadness about the matter. A form of
sadness that is a sickness. These people providing what they call opportunity, actually are
blind to the dictatorship they actually apply.
They are so morbidly constructed--under fear and
position seeking--that they've denounced their
human element. They exist in falsification and
dare not venture beyond the fail safe boundary
line. Meaning they refuse to step on anyone's
toe that held a higher position than they possess.

Here I was. A minority. A suppressed black.
A member of a race of people who thought they
would never possess manhood until they were ac-
cepted by the white race. And I, in all my shock
and bewilderment, stood courageously independent;
Truly a man.

Before leaving the program I talked with the managing editor, [publisher] Charles Gould. Many
at the *Examiner* viewed the abrupt fashion in which
I approached the situation as a confrontative act.
However, this was far from the authentic point.
I had to relay an experience to the man. How come
a man couldn't tell a story like it happened to
have been, instead of how it might force the
readers to react. Why was it his employees re-
fused to bring matters to him, yet greeted him
with smiling faces whenever he took his stroll
through the room of falsifications (Press Room).

It was here that I found shock and bewilderment.
Gould didn't know many of the things we elaborated
on. Nor could he, himself, understand the aliena-
tion between himself and the *Examiner* staff.

I don't doubt that Gould possesses his moody
sides, who among us doesn't. Yet when a working
condition is that of fear and suppressed animos-
ities there can never exist a human unity.

Therefore, I found in my brief affiliation with
the alleged "thinking" whites, a semi-concentra-
tion camp, one that I could never truly be a part
of.

I conversed at length with white men who were
emotionally destroyed as a result of publication
procedures. Men who acknowledged the need for
the news media to change its format and truly
relate to the people. And in the break of it
all I broke away, still hardcore, self-sustaining
and complete; leaving behind an image that I'm
sure will remain imprinted within the minds of
those affiliated with me.

INTERNS' VIEWS ON THE CHARGE OF INDOCTRINATION

Each intern was asked if he had read Byars's article and whether he agreed with the charge of indoctrination. Not all the interns had read the article, but
most had some feelings about indoctrination. It was
particularly difficult for them to distinguish between
outright indoctrination, and expectations by the paper
that a trainee would fit into an established method of
looking at events and an established method of writing
about them.

Louise Eubanks said, "Black people can be taught
to write a story the way you are supposed to. But what
Rufus is talking about...is that that's not the way we
are--it's just not going to work. I can't tell a story
in the inverted pyramid style about my people; I can
tell a story like that about white people....It's an
indoctrination of sorts--I know what he means--it's
just that our life styles are so different from theirs."

"Rufus had a point," said Hollis Wagstaff, "in that
when all the trainees come into this office they come
under an already existing system. And they come into
an environment that already has its own view of the
world....I wouldn't say it was indoctrination, I would
say you were being familiarized with the way that the
American newspaper views the world."

Many interns, although they expressed sympathy with
Byars's opinions, felt that the type of indoctrination
practiced by the *Examiner* was valid. They defined this
indoctrination as the teaching of writing standards and
standards of fair reportage. Jim Logan was one who
decided he fit into this definition of being indoctrinated. "I think it's essential that you conform to a
uniform journalistic style." After a reflective pause,
he added, "I guess because I have been partially indoctrinated."

Christopher Kabungura didn't call it indoctrination, and he thinks the system valid, but he did point out how the *Examiner*, like any other newspaper, manages to get its own viewpoint into print. "They would send you to cover stories they wanted covered. I don't know if there are some places they should have sent us that they didn't ....[but] the editing itself has nothing to do with indoctrination--it has to do with style. I don't see the relevance between editing and indoctrination."

Trina Chope matter-of-factly disagreed with the theory of indoctrination: "I think that's pretty silly. I guess because I respect both Al and Lynn and also because most of the people they hired had enough brains not to be indoctrinated that easily."

Several interns, who wished to remain anonymous on this point, spoke, not of indoctrination, but of a general feeling of oppression at the *Examiner*. One said, "There is a general oppressive air that everyone feels, not just the minority trainees. It's because of the reactionary policies of the publisher. Anyone would admit it, but not, maybe, to an outsider.

"It's a well-known inside fact, and it's really too bad, because it's a fine and talented staff, but no one can do his best there. That's part of the oppression that Rufus felt--I don't think he really attributed it to its source. I can really see where he would feel that way."

INTERNS LOOK AT PEOPLE, PRINCIPLES AND SPECIFICS

In the interviews, interns coupled specific criticisms, e.g., low pay, with expressed concern that the program should continue. Although they saw it as imperfect, they generally agreed that the program had value, and certainly that many staff members had at best met the challenge posed by training interns, or at least had tried to help: "Everybody here is eager to teach you .... reporters [were] cooperative and helpful and [we] even went out drinking with them ...."Lynn and Al used to bring around books which they sort of encouraged us to read .... they seemed to really try to communicate."

The interns characterized reporters: One was "a very good judge and sharp critic of writing"; another was seen as "a good investigative reporter--he makes you think." Finally, one intern who reported "very little racism," added, "You find what you look for."

As for evidence of racism, "It's nothing intentional, just a lack of experience in dealing with minorities and knowing the sorts of things that might offend." More somberly: "Some of the news and the way they play up news was very racist. That didn't hurt me individually, but it hurt me collectively as a Black person."

Interns also commented on a number of specifics, as well as the overall philosophy of the program.

Adequacy of Pay

Opinions about the adequacy of the internship pay varied, ranging from "Even if they had asked us to pay to be in that program, it still would have been a bargain," to indifference to the amount of pay, to an emphatic "No. It wasn't enough to live on." Some of those who found the pay inadequate still thought the benefits of the program outweighed any financial sacrifice. Dave Randolph said, "At the time, who cared? Just the idea of working on a newspaper, getting the experience, meeting people, being in the big league, was enough to compensate for the low pay I got."

Kieran Manjarrez thought it would be bad for the morale of reporters if trainees were paid at beginning reporter's scale. "Trainees shouldn't be paid at beginning reporter's scale because you have to think of the consequences...some reporter's bound to say, 'WHAT? That moron can't write a straight sentence and he's getting paid as much as I am.' That would create friction."

The low wage was an incentive, according to Richard Harris, who said, "Psychologically, I think it's best to keep it below a regular reporter's wages. I feel that you would perform more to try to get up to that salary. Getting a higher salary is a form of congratulations for finishing the training program." Trina Chope disagreed on principle: "It's not a matter of how much it takes to live on, though I think it is difficult for people to live on $65 a week, which is what we cleared. But it's a matter of when you pay people as copy boys you treat them as copy boys."

The trainees who gave up well-paying jobs to join the program were especially conscious of the problems of living on a low salary. Orville Springs, who left a job with take-home pay of $115 a week to join the program, felt he could qualify for welfare. Gail Christian had been a legal secretary, and found the intern salary inadequate. "I do live on it," she said, "but it's very difficult. I'm single. If I had a family I would have to turn them out." Jim Lee also took a big cut in salary, but he was able to extend his pay by knowledgeable use of the expense account. He too found the advantages of the program worth the cost: "I was making quite a bit less than when I was selling real estate, but... it's pretty cutthroat, and offers virtually no security unless you become a broker....I was doing something I enjoyed at the *Examiner*."

Extensions

Two of the trainees whose appointments were extended beyond 13 weeks complained of the difficulty of making plans in the face of the *Examiner's* indecision. Lena Baker, who received two extensions of four weeks each, said: "They wanted to keep me, but they wouldn't really tell me definitely that they would hire me. That way you are kind of just in limbo....It's terrible suspense for people--they don't know how to plan for the future." Trina Chope, who had the longest extension (20 weeks), said, "It was silly. It was all right for me because I didn't know what I wanted, but I think they should make up their minds. An extension should be for the benefit of the intern, in which case six weeks is plenty long. If interns are hired at all, it should be right after the six weeks."

Conflicting Criticisms by Staff Members

A few interns mentioned the fact that Cline, Ludlow, and the various reporters judged stories differently, and said they felt the different demands made by the different critics were confusing. Lon Daniels was one who experienced competing criticisms: "I think there were only two writing mechanisms that Cline ever mentioned to me: One was not to use 'that'--like 'he said that'--[the other was] not to start sentences with drop-bucket sentences--like "of more than 2,000 people at the meeting, Mrs. Brown said that the majority supported her.' He said we don't talk like that. One time I had taken out all the 'thats,' and Ludlow said to put them back in. I said, 'But so-and-so told me....' Ludlow said, 'I know, sometimes I put his back in, too.'"

Independence

As noted, the second group of interns was asked to do a special project or "term paper." Susan Almazol did hers on the Filipino community in San Francisco, and commented, "At the time we complained about it a lot. I think it took more knowledge than I had and I was very dissatisfied with the end product. I didn't know the sources of information, etc. Lynn rearranged things so it looked a lot better than I had written it."

Patel questioned the value of the term paper. He
thought the interns should be exposed to deadline pressure a lot earlier, and suggested that one day a week
the interns should be turned loose and told to go out
and dig up a story on their own. Another supporter of
the idea of turning interns loose to dig up their own
stories was Lon Daniels: "If I was running the program
I would handle it pretty much the way Lynn and Cline
did, only I would stress going out and getting a story
on your own. I would stress that very early in the
program. I would just tell the trainees to bring in
something at least once a week. That's what really makes
you a success in journalism--what you bring in from outside, not something that is assigned to you. Something
that you know and tell about."

Supervision

Most of the interns thought that, in general there
was adequate supervision. Some found it inadequate for
themselves; others said that while they felt they personally had been given sufficient direction and assistance, there was not enough guidance for the program as
a whole.

Rufus Byars felt there was no supervision at all:
"Not enough for me to learn, if they really wanted me
to learn the journalistic pros and cons that they dealt
with." Gregory Gross, who found the supervision inadequate, said, "The people responsible for supervision
had other responsibilities and it's darn near impossible
for a newspaperman to go too many ways at once....People
have talked about this lack of supervision as if it
was deliberate on the part of the *Examiner*, and I don't
think it was. There's just too much work to be done."

Gail Christian felt there was not really enough
supervision "for somebody who didn't have some discipline
and wasn't used to the eight-hour day. You took the
responsibility of doing what you knew you were supposed

to do until somebody had time. Is that really supervision?....And there should be a minority [person] somewhere in that Ludlow-Cline-Cook team; it would run a
lot smoother." Lena Baker said, "Each individual person
has different needs. Myself, I really don't care for
a lot of supervision....But for some people, younger,
more inexperienced persons, it probably wouldn't have
been well enough structured."

Leslie McBee found a way to get the help needed.
"It's very loosely supervised and if you are not the
kind of person who's going to badger them, you will
probably sit at your desk. I didn't give them the opportunity to just let me sit there. I had a lot of questions. A less outgoing person might have problems with
this program."

Several interns noted the heavy pressure on Lynn
Ludlow and pointed out the need for a full- or part-time
supervisor. As Lena Baker pointed out, "Lynn really
had a lot to do. They never gave him any special time
to devote to it, and they really can't expect people
to be that altruistic." Trina Chope thought it would
be best if there were a full-time supervisor. "I think
the people that were supervising were a very good combination because most people could get along with one
or the other....A full-time supervisor or two half-time
ones would be best."

Discrimination and Racism

The interns reported that they encountered very
little personal expression of racism at the *Examiner*.
Hollis Wagstaff remarked, "Discrimination? Uh-uh, not
in the office. I didn't meet that at all. This is not
to say any very covert strain wasn't there, but I didn't
meet any. This was very surprising. A friend asked me
just after I started the program: 'How is that racist
S.F. *Examiner* treating you?' And I said, 'Fine, fine.'"

Others who spoke of racism felt it was inherent in the program. Rufus Byars said: "I didn't encounter any overt racism. Surreptitiously, yes; you can't even deal with me on a racist issue because you're too involved trying to break my independence....As long as we exist, there isn't any program where whites can train Blacks. Superior and inferior is the white way of life; as long as it's that way, you can't deal with it. There's no such thing as me coming into your cancer and creating another cancer--all I can do is receive cancer."

Lance Gilmer said: "I think they should abolish the program or quit having it be such a racist thing. There are only 1.7 percent of the reporters or journalists in the country who are Black. On this paper you see one male Black--that's me....Let's face it--they know there are no jobs out there....They don't want Black journalists out there or there wouldn't be only 1.7 percent....I'm not putting Lynn down; Lynn and Al are sincere....But it's the whole program. Any time you hear of a program for Blacks, you know it's a rip-off.

"I'm not trying to change a racist attitude--all I want is to be able to function as a human being.... What's happening now is reverse racism, but I'm still a commodity."

Kieran Manjarrez also referred to the program as reverse racism: "It's no discredit to the program, but I think there is such a thing as inverse racism--any program like this is inversely racist. You're looking for people that are Black and good, rather than good and Black. That makes you racist because your primary concern is a racist thing."

IV

The Program's Impact on the Examiner

The training program carried potential impact in two directions: the first on the lives and attitudes of the interns, and the second, on the staff of the *Examiner*. Did the second force become a reality? To sound out participants, reporters, the managing editor, the city editor, the publisher and trainees were asked to comment on whether the program had effected any increase in sensitivity in the writing and editing of the paper, or influenced the reporters themselves.

VIEWS FROM THE STAFF SIDE

With respect to changes in staff attitudes, Ed Dooley, managing editor of the *Examiner*, commented that as a result of the merger and realignment of the San Francisco papers his paper had lost nearly all the young people on the staff. He felt that the intern program had made staff reporters more sensitive and more aware, and that this change included the older people. "I've found this true of myself, a lot of us have around here," he said. "We didn't bother to go out and really visit Hunters Point and the Fillmore areas. A lot of desk people have been strapped down to the desk." He also thought there had been a difference in the coverage.

"...a very positive difference over the past five years. We were already turned around, I think, and were

trying to do a more intensive and straightforward reporting job. This program continued and perhaps made a
broader base of awareness within the staff itself.

"It's certainly here to stay at this paper....It's
going to continue if I have anything to say about it,
and I have quite a bit to say about it. From the self-
ish point of view, here's a market of young people that's
practically handed to us on a platter. We have to do
some training, but there's nothing wrong with that. I
would think other newspapers would try it. After all,
newspapers are always looking for bright young people
to come on their staffs and this is certainly one way
to build."

Also mentioning the age difference, Jim Schermerhorn
said: "After the merger we had an average age on our
staff of about 50. It was nice having young people
around for 13 and more weeks where they weren't under
pressure to be hired; they were not like other young
employees who after 13 weeks didn't make it. But it's
of benefit to us to have some extremely bright young
people around whom we could enjoy because we didn't have
to suffer through the trial period with them. They
continually brought new ideas into the office and exposed
the office to an age we had been missing for three or
four years.

"We were exposed to something highly unusual on a
metropolitan paper. Metropolitan papers usually sit
around and wait for somebody who has been a star on
some smaller paper for a few years--somebody 10 years
out of school--and even so, half of them wind up going
back to being stars in their smaller communities.
Here we enjoyed youngsters much younger, members of the
generation that has been very much in the news. They
have been able to work with us despite the very strong
barriers of age and in some cases feelings of being a
member of a minority. Despite this they found that they
could have some liking and respect for some of the members of the staff. A friend of mine, an assistant editor

of the New York *Times*, said the generation gap has affected the *Times*'s hiring in that they suspect they're not getting the same caliber of young people who were once coming to them. The valuable ones have let their hair grow and are traveling and seeking something far better to do in life than joining the Establishment. I think we created this thing and bumbled along with it in a most unprofessional manner, but we have had around us some young people whose personal feelings of loyalty to the staff sort of overcame their ideas about the Establishment. And some of them, I think, found that they could indeed make an impression."

The impact has been personal for Schermerhorn, too: "One of the deepest personal values to me is that it helped me in my continued evaluation of the newspaper life and my role in it--and I'm a seventh generation newspaperman--and the constant question of whether I should stay in it, with the merger and advertising monopoly, to learn its new role in the community.

"I've seen responsible newspapers in a small community where there was only one newspaper. This lacks some of the dash of the old newspaper days, but it can be extremely satisfying to feel you are living up to a grave responsibility to do something about the new problems--not the dishonest cop or the old problems that have always been with us. The last two big newspaper stories have been discrimination, and, evolving out of that, the revolution. In some ways we have done darn poorly, and in some ways damn well. In the old days, if you disagreed with the city editor, you could throw a typewriter at him and then go to work across the street. And get a $10 raise while you were at it, if you were lucky. But there's no street to cross anymore, so you must fight your battles and stay where you are.

"Talking to young people and trying to explain the newspaper business has helped me, I think, in my re-evaluation of my role. It helped me at least to decide to stay and try to work under these new conditions. The newsroom looks a little more like the streets of San Francisco. It's certainly not the mixture that we would like and ought to have, but it's better. As far as changing or improving our program goes, I think the important thing is to keep it. I think we owe it to ourselves to see that our editorial room reflects the racial makeup of the country."

Another *Examiner* reporter who felt the impact of the program on a personal level was Mary Crawford, who said: "I learn more about communicating by teaching the newswriting class than I learned at Columbia getting an M.A. in journalism. As far as the young people are concerned, we are not communicating with many of them on what they call the Establishment newspapers. I think my coverage has actually changed. For instance, instead of just covering some event at Alcatraz, you cover what actually happened and then you interpret it from the viewpoint of the Alcatraz Indian leaders, the council members.

"Eventually if you cover the same kind of story, you can figure it out for yourself anyway, but working with the minorities, if you're not a minority, just speeds up this process."

Reporter Jim Wood added, "I think it does serve as an educational process in the newsroom for people not in the program. I think this is particularly true of some of the executives who I think don't have much contact ordinarily with the minority community."

EVALUATION BY THE PUBLISHER

Publisher Charles Gould observed that the program has had some impact on the *Examiner*, too:

I feel the program has been good for the *Examiner*.
I hope it has been good for the interns. Through
direct involvement with the interns, our reporters and editors udoubtedly achieved a better
understanding of minority problems while being
made more aware of the talents and capabilities
of many members of minority groups.

The training program has had an impact on department heads as well as on reporters, and I am sure
we are now taking a longer look at some issues
in the minority communities than we did before
the program started. This is good.

Newspaper coverage of racial matters has, of
course, gone through dramatic changes during the
last 10 or 15 years. This is not peculiar to the
Examiner. It has happened on many publications
and is a reflection of the awakening--long over-
due--of our collective social conscience. If
the *Examiner* has moved faster in some areas than
other newspapers it is probably because of two
circumstances: (1) We are in a supersensitive,
supersophisticated, socially conscious community;
and (2) we have the minority training program--
and its architects--as part of our operation.

I believe the infusion of more and more minority
journalists into the mainstream of publishing
and communications will strengthen our profession,
our system and our nation. If our program gives
even a slight nudge in this direction it is worthwhile.

I do not believe Negro reporters should concen-
trate exclusively on racial issues and social
problems. Each minority member who joins the
staff should be considered as a part of the total team covering the total community. However,

I can understand the logic that moves a white editor to assign a Negro reporter to a racial or
ethnic story and thus have the paper benefit
through the reporter's built-in expertise in such
matters.

I feel a newspaper should be a mirror of the community it serves. It should concern itself with
the problems of all its people.

There are probably cross-pollination benefits in
having white reporters cover issues in the black
community. However, there should not be hard and
fast rules in this regard. In fact, I think it
would be unfortunate if newspapers should fragment
and weaken their staffs by making assignments on
the basis of race or color. You do not develop
togetherness through divisiveness.

TRAINEES' COMPLAINTS

As reporter Al Cline pointed out however, "We
haven't gotten into the real problems of changing the
newspaper to where it's responsive, at least a little
bit, to the various communities. I just don't think
anybody is making enough of an effort. I do think we
have learned an awful lot about minority people--at
least some people have, I hope."

Two complaints by trainees illustrate Cline's point.
Gregory Gross recalled:

The only incident that disturbed me was an almost-
editorial dealing with the rising murder toll in
San Francisco last year. Part of the story was
a boxed insert which was a composite murderer
based on statistics: He is more often Black than
white and rarely Oriental, and it went on to say

that he is often a homosexual. At the end of the story Captain Martin Lee was quoted; he more or less attached the execution-type murders to the hate teachings of the Black Panther Party. What upset me about this was the obvious racial overtones of it and the fact that most of these murders were unsolved. Trina verbally assaulted Gale [Cook], who agreed with her. I wrote a pretty nasty letter to the editor, which was printed. The editor replied that crimes are committed by individuals, and not by races, which was fine, but I thought that could have been brought out in the story more. That was the only one. Black people often read into white people's stories a good deal--they look for traces of racism and often find it. In the program we learn how they think and they learn how we think, and I think we will both be better off.

Gail Christian was upset by at least one *Examiner* story, too, and sounded less forgiving. "They tell you that it's important that a journalist report fairly-- and then they turn around and do things that are so terrible on the front page of their newspaper." She cited a story in the summer of 1970, when several Black teen-agers, apparently feeling over-exuberant at the close of school, roughed up a few innocent bus passengers and broke a few windows. "The *Examiner*," said Gail, "had huge headlines proclaiming 'Vicious Black Gang Hits Stonestown' and a story on 'Black guerrilla band.' So, you almost have to go the other way to balance it out."

Louise Eubanks discussed the problems of insensitivity at some length:

There were times when the way they would cover a story involving Black people would make me upset or anxious, and I would go to the reporter and say, "Look what you have done or said." Sometimes someone would ask me to read his story and tell

him what I thought and I would tell him, straight
out, what I thought. I didn't spare his feelings.
When he made a statement that Blacks could mis-
read, I would say, "You just have to understand
that I'm an emotional Black woman and this is
what I read into what you wrote. I don't care
what you meant."

Many of them said it was valuable for us to be
there; many of them had never been talked to
about their own feelings on racism. I found that
I would go home at night exhausted from verbal-
izing with them when I felt they needed to be
talked to about things, and I had to do something
to reach them. It was a learning experience for
them in that way....Rufus mentioned something
about feeling they were picking his brains. He's
correct in thinking this; I know what he means.
But that's part of the situation--communication.
I think our silence is one place we've gone wrong
with white people; we needed to holler out a long
time ago to let them know where they've hurt us
and are still hurting us. The frustration is that
they don't *really* listen. If they do, we don't
know it.

V

Assessments and Some Conclusions

ALAN CLINE ON MINORITY EMPLOYMENT

Alan Cline has worked consistently on the training program since its inception, and was one of the founders of the Newsmen's Job Referral Committee that initiated the original petition to Publisher Gould. He was asked for his views on intern programs and their relationship to minority employment in newspapers, and responded as follows:

Those of us working in The *Examiner's* intern program these past three years are well aware of its limitations, of its less than adequate scope.

We would agree, I think, with almost all of what is said, or at least much of what is reported in Mrs. Telfer's interviews.

What needs attention far more than the paltry efforts of one newspaper is the lack of commitment of the entire industry. At the top.

No intern program will succeed without jobs at the end. There must be adequate commitment on the part of management so adequate time for helping the trainee, teaching if you will, is available.

There must be a realization that intern programs by their very nature lead to frustration. They have to. Any time adults are thrown into a foreign situation and want desperately to succeed within a ridiculously short period, tensions are certain to surface.

Our interns wanted to make it. They sweated over stories and fumed at themselves at what they considered their own inadequacies. It was not enough to compare my 20 years' experience with their week or two. They wanted to be good newsmen.

And what did they find at the end of the road?

The Associated Press comes up with tests, on vocabulary, on some kind of trash I.Q. test that a university graduate fluent in four languages manages to fail. It was agreed he could write, but there were those tests. It was a dodge to maintain the status quo.

UPI always is cutting back. Publishers and editors make much noise about doing something, but when they are asked to deliver, economics manages to get in the way.

There is no commitment for any kind of change. Look at the Bay Area press. Inadequate though it may be, The *Examiner* remains the only paper, major or minor, doing anything. A giant like the *Chronicle* says they cannot afford an intern program.

No one at the top in the media is saying that perhaps changes should be made because a broader representation in the city rooms would lead to a better product. I doubt that anyone is saying, dammit, it just isn't right to maintain such isolated staffs. This is 1971, time for change.

It is fitting and proper to editorialize about
fair employment, about the necessity for everyone else to open their doors, about ending discrimination of every kind. But do as I say, not
as I do.

So we can discuss forever the relative merits
of this kind of intern program versus that kind.
But until the people in the position to make some
changes decide to do so, we're beating the dead-
est of horses.

Alan D. Cline

Berkeley, California
November 30, 1971

To my knowledge, there has been no change since
this was written. The 1971 statement still
stands.

A.D.C.

January 15, 1973

DRAWING UP A BALANCE SHEET

In the foregoing pages, participants in the *Examiner's* minority intern training program have reviewed
their experiences and given their judgments. In addition, it may be useful for an observer to offer some
evaluations and recommendations that seek to combine
their reports with some personal interpretations.

Recruitment: Some Inadequacies and Alternatives

As Lynn Ludlow noted, recruitment procedures are
inadequate on at least two counts: They may be failing

to reach a broad enough sample of prospects, and at the same time may risk the danger of over-recruiting. For the second hazard, he is concerned about having to turn applicants away when he has no real alternative to offer. The evening newswriting class is, however, a viable alternative, and applicants who cannot qualify, or who cannot be included in a current program because of lack of space, should be encouraged to enroll. In fact, for interns to derive the greatest possible benefit from the program, the class should be considered a prerequisite for anyone lacking an adequate command of the fundamentals.

More vigorous and widespread recruitment may well necessitate telling applicants that there is no room for some of them, or that they need further education in order to qualify. But it would permit the *Examiner* to select interns from a broader and perhaps different sample of applicants. Further, increased public recruitment would help funnel to the *Examiner* young professionals who are stuck in their present jobs and want to move on.

Another problem touches on recruitment: the determination of which minority persons should be eligible for the program. In a direct response to the findings of the National Advisory Commission on Civil Disorders, the *Examiner* program was established to increase employment of all minorities represented in the urban American community, so that all might receive more effective and more sensitive news coverage. This is an admirable goal, and the inclusion of Americans of Mexican, Chinese, Japanese, Filipino, Indian, Black or any other descent characterized as minority is entirely proper. But it seems clear that the *Examiner* is only diffusing its efforts when it includes foreign visitors who have no plans to remain and become permanent residents. (This is not in any way to belittle the ability or personal qualities of those foreign interns who were included in the group of 21 interviewed. It is instead an attempt to insure that a necessarily limited effort pays off directly for the resident American community.)

I believe that the problem being tackled by the *Examiner* program is primarily that of American racism. It follows, therefore, that membership in an American racial minority should be a primary qualification for admission to the minority intern program.

With respect to commitment and preparation of the interns, any applicant who is not reasonably certain of commitment to the field of journalism should also be requested to take the class in newswriting. If he shows dedication and ability, he could then be admitted to the training program. The class thus has the potential for providing basic training in the fundamentals of writing and techniques and functioning as a test of an applicant's commitment. The class is large enough to accommodate people who have not made up their minds about the profession; the training program is not.

To accept interns who have not yet learned the fundamentals is more than just a waste of time for the *Examiner;* the result is often frustration, discouragement, or anger on the part of the young people. Unless the program is drastically changed and extended, it should accept only those who already have the basic tools of English and need only to learn the techniques of newswriting or gain practical experience.

Thus, it seems clear that the internship program cannot be aimed at the "hard-core" unemployed. As it is now organized, the program cannot start from scratch and teach sufficient skills to produce journalists in 13 weeks. Perhaps the composing room or other functional areas of the newspaper plant could inaugurate training programs of their own to tackle this problem.

Minority persons with journalism degrees do not need the intern program training any more than do whites with journalism degrees, or, really, minorities with degrees in other fields. Some newspapers have consistently hired individuals with degrees in fields other than journalism. But the program presumably does offer a way to enter the newspaper business, and here minorities need all the help they can get.

Supervision: Strengths and Weaknesses

The program's loose structure is both a strength
and a weakness: It allows self-starters to do their
best, but it fails those who need guidance and direction.
To serve the needs of individual interns, the program
requires a half-time supervisor, a reporter who has
been relieved of some of his other duties.   Supervision
is acutely needed in the first and last few weeks of
the program.   During the first weeks, interns need help
until they have become accustomed to the routine, and
feel sufficiently at home to ask questions.   And, during
the last few weeks, the supervisor must handle job re-
ferrals and placement.

As Ludlow noted, supervisory tasks make heavy demands on time and energy.   He and Cline have thus far
expended most of the energy required to start the program
and keep it running; Ludlow, at least, seems to show
signs of battle fatigue.   If the program is to be continued indefinitely, as all levels at the *Examiner* have
agreed that it should, the load should be shared.

The all-important drive needed to prove that the
program could work has come largely from Ludlow; in fact,
without him there probably would never have been a minority training program at the *Examiner*.   It seems clear
that Ludlow and Cline should now be enabled to share
much of their supervisory responsibility with the rest
of the *Examiner* staff, perhaps retaining control of
scheduling and overall supervision.

Ideally, the supervision of trainees in their day-
to-day work should be rotated among members of the city
room staff and other reporters.   Trainees could be
"checked out" to different reporters for a day or a week
at a time.   In such a system, each reporter would be
totally responsible for his trainee during that assignment period.

A system of changing supervisors would undoubtedly result in uneven training; some reporters are naturally better teachers than others. But the trainees would benefit from the variety, and all members of the staff would feel they were participating in the program they helped bring about when they signed the petition to Publisher Gould. The trainees should be warned that they will be given conflicting statements of fact and must learn through trial and error which to retain and which to discard. This experience would prepare them for the reality of writing for different editors.

The trainees should not only follow the reporter on the story; they should write the parallel story, read the account the reporter turns in, and show their own story to the reporter. Individual reporters must learn something of the art of criticizing trainees' stories; the trainees' final stories might be submitted to Cline or Ludlow for final approval.

Some trainees have not been sent out on beats, but beat coverage should be reinstated in subsequent programs. A combination of covering beats and spending time in other departments seems to have been an enriching experience. The intern should get at least a taste of as many aspects of the newspaper business as possible so that he can see the range of alternatives to straight news reporting on the cityside.

Indefinite Extensions: Who Benefits?

The intern is kept dangling during indefinite job extensions, while hiring decisions are being made. Meanwhile, the paper benefits from the services of an eager reporter. In fairness to the interns, extensions should be limited to a specific maximum: possibly four or six weeks.

The Problem of Pay and Subsidy

The present wage for interns is probably adequate
for single people. Some trainees professed not to care
about the money because they were doing what they wanted
to do and felt that the benefits were worth the sacrifice. However, virtually every trainee who was the family's principal wage earner felt that the pay was not
enough to live on, and was insufficient to feed a family.
To accomplish the objective of the program, to induce
more minority people to go into journalism, some subsidy
should be provided for interns with dependents so that
they are not starved out of the program.

Jim Schermerhorn noted, "We have seen people in
their early 30's whom we liked very much and wanted in
the program, but they have to be concerned about feeding
their children at the same time." He lamented the present impossibility of one hopeful solution: "It would
be nice if the unions would step in and give them [the
interns] some extra money, but with the *Herald-Examiner*
strike down in Southern California, they just don't
have it." (The local Newspaper Guild has made it possible for all interns to become members of the local
by paying their national dues and forgiving payment of
local dues.)

In the meantime, the *Examiner* should pay additional
"living expenses" to trainees with dependents (probably
$20-$40 per week), or should search for an alternative
solution such as grants from other sources. In the
absence of such a supplement, the program will fail to
attract talented people who would like to become journalists but are unwilling to sacrifice their families' well-
being in order to do so.

The Employment Picture

From the beginning, interns should be informed that
the Bay Area job market for reporters is extremely

competitive, and that their chances of finding employment will be increased if they are willing to move out
of the area. Nevertheless, the experiences of the interns indicated that wherever they go job-hunting--small
town daily, Bay Area newspaper, or "the country's better
newspapers"--some jobs seem to be available for those
interns who diligently seek them.

Is the *Examiner* Listening?

The original letter to Publisher Charles Gould from
the *Examiner* staff, soliciting his support for a program,
contained a quote from the Kerner Report:

"If the media are to report with understanding,
wisdom and sympathy on the problem of the cities and the
problems of the black man--for the two are increasingly
intertwined--they must employ, promote and *listen* to
Negro journalists." [emphasis added] Judging by the
examples cited in Chapter IV, the full *Examiner* staff
has not yet adequately learned how to listen. There
appears to be some increased sensitivity developing out
of the program, but much more is apparently needed at
all levels.

Many of the trainees recognize their responsibility
to talk "to them [the reporters] about their own feelings
on racism" and let them "know where they've hurt us and
are still hurting us." Gregory Gross and Gail Christian,
for example, commented on stories and headlines that
they recognized as inciting or exploiting race fear and
hatred. When the *Examiner* journalists, or those of any
paper, hear and understand the messages of minority
trainees, such headlines and stories will disappear and
become merely grotesque mementos of the past.

CONCLUSION: WAITING FOR THE NEXT STEPS

The *Examiner* program is an honest attempt, certainly on the part of those most intimately involved, to solve the problems of communication with minority communities. It has added at least nine members to the ranks of working minority journalists, some of whom would not be journalists at all were it not for the program.

As Schermerhorn noted, it has been a "bumbling, unprofessional" program; the *Examiner* has made many of the inevitable mistakes, but it has learned from them. This experience has been valuable for both the *Examiner* and the other newspapers that may be inspired to begin programs of their own.

The real test however, is not just how many minority persons can be trained for and hired by the news media, but further, how many will find American journalism tolerable enough on the inside to stay with it.

The point was made by Louise Eubanks:

It seems to me that the final telling point of these programs is how many Black reporters stay on after they have been hired. How long do they stay and what are their reasons for leaving? A follow-up in five years would be necessary.

It's just that we are tired of fighting the pressure of our skin color plus the other frustrations of a job....The whole aspect of writing is such an emotional thing. And then you have got to always worry about this part of you because the editor fails somehow to make you valid as a human being because your skin is Black--it's just really very heavy.

The need for minority representatives on American newspapers is indisputable. But as Alan Cline pointed out in his statement, there remains "the lack of commitment of the entire industry. At the top."

Finally, it is harder to evaluate a continuing process, like the *Examiner's* intern program than, for example, a completed project that can be seen whole and in perspective. At the same time, the fact that intern training is still alive and appears to be an integral part of the *Examiner's* activity program must be recognized as a signal of success and stamina: It involves demanding work undertaken out of personal commitment and without the sweetening of outside funds. Staff members, executives and interns have been open in their criticisms of staffing levels, wages, intern selection and supervision, and almost every other aspect of the program, but a reader can detect even in the criticisms an undercurrent of conviction that the program is worthwhile and hope that it will flourish.

Conflicting and contradictory opinions abound, particularly with respect to the availability of jobs. The program can recruit and train, but admittedly it cannot create job openings. Still, its inability to solve single-handedly the employment problem for minority journalists does not detract from its demonstrated capacity to make contact with promising young minority men and women, to give them training and a chance to develop professional skills, and to suggest for other professional journalists a fresh insight into people and neighborhoods in the city they thought they already knew.

Beyond this, as Lynn Ludlow has indicated, the program avoids elaborate justification. It aspires only to be "a good idea"--and one that seems to be working. This realism and refusal to inflate a modest program with a high-sounding prospectus suggest some of the program's major strengths: a continuing trial-and-error approach, a bias toward candor, and a willingness to keep on trying to do what is "right."

VI

Interviews with the Interns

In a minority intern training program, the interns themselves are in the spotlight; they are constantly observing, adjusting, learning, teaching and reacting, and of course, being observed. Of all the opinions and reactions, theirs are central to the success or failure of the program. Consequently, each of the 21 interns who participated in the program through early 1971 was interviewed in depth in interview sessions lasting from one to two hours each. As indicated below, the same questions were put to each intern, with opportunity to comment on areas beyond the specifics of the questions. The three interns who were out of state at the time of the study each received a questionnaire and explanatory letter, followed by a half-hour telephone interview.

Excerpts and quotes from some of the interviews have appeared on previous pages. Because of the intrinsic interest in the interns' responses, as many as possible of their additional comments are included in the following section. Some cuts have been made, but the words are those of the interns themselves.

QUESTIONS ASKED

Following are the questions asked in each of the intern interviews. Key words in parentheses are used as guides in the section "The Interns and Their Answers." For answers to the first two questions, see the section on "Who Are the Interns and What Are They Doing Now?" (pp. 5-8). For a more inclusive listing of page references to topics discussed in the questions and answers, see the "Partial Index," pp. 123-124.

What was your education and journalism background?

How did you come to apply to the program? (Recruitment)

Do you feel the pay was adequate? (Pay)

Describe the types of activities you performed while a trainee. Did you work in various departments at the *Examiner*? Which? (Assignments)

How many of your stories were published in the *Examiner* during the program? How many bylines did you receive? (Bylines)

Were you kept on as a cub reporter at the end of the program? (Time Extension)

Did you feel supervision was adequate during the program? (Supervision)

Do you approve/disapprove of the reduction in the number of trainees from four to two? (Trainee Reduction)

How would you characterize the attitude of *Examiner* staffers and supervisors: fair, sincere, condescending, outrageous? (Staff Attitude)

Do you feel the program was indoctrination rather than merely training? (Indoctrination Charge)

Were you given assistance in finding a job? (Job Placement)

Do you feel the *Examiner* program adequately trained you for a reporter's job? (Professional Training)

How would you evaluate the program? (Evaluation)

THE INTERNS AND THEIR ANSWERS

SUSAN ALMAZOL, interviewed at the UC Berkeley campus, March 2, 1970: (Note: Although she permitted me to use quotes extracted from her interview, she preferred that the interview itself not be included. J.T.)

LENA BAKER, interviewed at the San Francisco *Chronicle*, February 25, 1970:

Pay

I managed to get along on it, but it's not adequate. I think if it's at all possible, they should be able to clear at least $100 a week. But it probably wasn't that bad for the newspaper business, compared to reporters. I think salaries in the newspaper business should be upgraded generally.

Assignments

I was in the women's section for one week—deathly. They had me copying recipes. It was one of the worst parts, but it didn't last too long. Then I went on the city hall beat for two weeks as a vacation replacement, but I was never systematically exposed to the beats as they promised. The beats are deadly dull. I like it in the newsroom. From an educational standpoint it would probably be better if people were exposed to the beats, but eventually you learn what they are all about. It's a soft, cushy sort of job, but it's just dull unless you have the Berkeley beat or something like that.

Bylines

They were quite lavish with bylines there [at the
Examiner]--much more than the *Chronicle* is. I
worked on a five-part series on welfare in San
Francisco. It was something I took up on my own
and they gave me all the time I needed. Unfortunately, it never got published. Gale said they
really wanted to publish it, but by the time they
decided they wanted to use it, Nixon's speech on
welfare had come out. They thought it would be
anticlimactic to run it then. I thought that
was sort of a flimsy excuse. I called for sweeping reforms--I guess they took it that Nixon was
proposing these sweeping reforms. Rush's [Rush
Greenlee] problems contributed to my quitting
there. If you can't have that freedom to be a
journalist, it's pretty bad.

Trainee Reduction

Supposedly they did it because it would be easier
with two people, which is true. But the question
arises, why don't they get more people in to supervise? All these programs have their faults--
KQED's supervisor devotes half time to the program. You have to have someone there who can really devote at least half of their time if they're
going to call it a training program.

I'm just sorry to hear it's been cut back. That's
all I can say.

Staff Attitude

Sincere, with a couple of exceptions, and they
don't really count; all the rest of the people at
the *Examiner* were really great. There weren't
any petty jealousies when I got a byline.

Job Placement

I got the job here at the *Chronicle* all on my own.
Sort of a contrary thing to do. I think they were
quite unhappy at my actions, but I felt that I had
a perfect right to go where I pleased. They
shouldn't think of me as some sort of traitor.
Some people really feel that way, I've heard.
There's some over-sensitivity on the part of some
of the people connected with the program as far as
criticism goes. But I think an effort is better
than no effort and it's good to get people employed in the field. The politics of the *Examiner*
aren't relevant, since trainees won't be working
there. There should be definitely more effort
made to follow up trainees afterwards; again, that
calls for someone to give part time to the program, and to establish a better job-finding appa-
ratus. Lynn is working on it but it's really a
big job. It's really weak at that point. The
Chronicle is the only place I applied, and I had
no real difficulty. But I would say that's the
exception rather than the rule.

Professional Training

I think [I had it]...although you are constantly
learning. I think it gave me an adequate base.
I had to learn a different style of writing--the
Chronicle has its own unique style.

Evaluation

I think it's a good program that needs improvement.

RUFUS BYARS, interviewed at his home in San Francisco, March 6, 1970:

> I'm self-educated. I had some college courses,
> but no high school degree. I wouldn't take
> journalism courses if I could. Those who are at
> the *Examiner* now are the ones that really need
> to be trained.

Recruitment

> I heard about it through an old affiliation of
> mine--a social worker. He told me to go down and
> check it out. I went down and showed them an
> autobiographical, philosophical, psychological
> piece I wrote.

Pay

> I wasn't really concerned with the pay. I did
> think they should pay trainees more if they have
> families, but if they don't have families, I don't
> think higher pay would be necessary. The real
> compensation is the ability to do your thing.
> They should pay an intern where he can sustain
> himself and his family.

Assignments

> I started out with obits, which bored me to death;
> from there to going out on stories on my own. I
> was there two weeks and I went out on a feature
> story of my own. It appeared in the Sunday supple-
> ment and there was a big debate on whether to
> give me a byline--I had moved too fast. Sometimes
> it's better just to throw a baby in the water and
> let him swim. I didn't get a byline on the story.

> I didn't find the critiques valuable. I didn't
> get anything out of the *Examiner* program except

hypocrisy. But I got a look at how people are
really functioning inside that newsroom. I just
got an inside look into the structure of mechan-
icalism. No one had any initiative or did anything on their own. I was there two months and
wanted to start a series on the high schools in
the city. All they did was sit on it, but told
me it was all right. They just wanted to keep
me out of their way.

Bylines

Everything I ever wrote was published. I did a
thing on the AMA, good reporting piece, just
straight, no personal opinions or interpretations. But no bylines. My first byline was at
the *Sun-Reporter*.

Time Extension

I was on police beat one week. It was morbid.
I was kept on for an extra month. I wanted to
be kept on. There was a big cantankerous debate:
I was an innovation to the Black training program. I was the type of Black that they always
claimed they were looking for, a hard-core arro-
gant Black personality, and independent. I went
in there and talked to Gould about my dissatis-
faction and after that I was kept on a little
while. My training period was merely a debate.
I don't really think that white America is truly
ready to deal with the personality that's not
following in its footsteps, but which still possesses what they proclaim intelligence. They
didn't want to accept me after reading my auto-
biography. Lynn told me after reading the first
two pages that we don't deal in things like this.
Nothing changes out there; it's always the same.
I know what's going on out there.

Supervision

Blacks were there so that the *Examiner* could say,
"We got Blacks on the staff." They say, "It's
hard for a white reporter to go into a Black
community." Any Black man with common sense would
acknowledge that he's being used. They'll tell
you what to say.

Trainee Reduction

When you have to go into details about how it is,
you run into problems. I wrote it [the *Ball &
Chain* article] so that they will have a mirror.
I think maybe they had forgot their true reflection.

Staff Attitude

The majority of my time was spent in the glad-
iators' pits. They were trying to misconstrue my
meanings. They would often tell me I should get
away from newspaper work and get into magazines
and novels. I was taking it as an experience.
Right now I'm trying to get an article in *The
Nation* on the Black press. I'm going through a
hassle right now because he can't accept what I
say. He's trying to pay me for my time, but I
don't want my pay until my article is published.

The Black press also suffers the same ills twice
over because they're trying to impress the white
establishment papers. When I came to the *Sun-
Reporter,* almost everything they had was a rewrite from the *Examiner.* In a month I had changed
all that. Once they found out I was writing
it like it was, well, it didn't work. The *Examiner* had been pinning up all my articles. Of
all the trainees they had, no one has come up
as fast as I have. I have an article coming out
in *Time* on Black poets. They take no credit

for that. Now I'm on my own and I'm going on into my own bag--metaphysics. The guy who wrote *Escape from Alcatraz* called me the Black Jack London. I have an article in 13 Communist newspapers--an article on a Black man's art gallery, from the *Sun*. They picked it up. I've been invited to have dinner with the Russian consulate, me and my family. The Panther paper has too much propaganda. Black newspapers are too conservative. I've got to tell people the truth.

Indoctrination Charge

There is nothing here in this country that's not indoctrination. I didn't say it was only a Black indoctrination.

Job Placement

I left the *Examiner* to go directly to the *Sun-Reporter*, with a front page story the first day. Jim Schermerhorn is the only one I hold any respect for--him and Al Cline. They lined up interviews, etc. "He's complicated"--Ludlow's terminology of my structure.

I was talking at one time with Tom Flemings, city editor at the *Sun-Reporter*, and he was very impressed with my ideological convictions at that time. However, he changed. I guess he figured I would come in and be a good boy, but it was ego that destroyed my desire to work for the Black press. Everybody was dying to impress, and then when I started getting too much recognition from the public...

Professional Training

I had applied at the *Sun-Reporter* nine months before the program. They wouldn't hire me then because I didn't have a name. It helped me get in,

if that was what I wanted.   Gave me my membership to fight for the ego.

Evaluation

Black people have been saying they were going to
get into the white man's game and then take over--
it's a myth.   White man can't make it in the jungle.   All the jungle would do to him would be to
absorb him.   I don't buy integration.   All we need
is communication.

TRINA CHOPE, interviewed at her home in Berkeley,
March 11, 1970:

Pay

It was adequate for me, but no, as a general principle I don't think it's adequate.   I think they
should be paying as close to a starting reporter's
salary as possible.

Recruitment

My biggest objection--and it did a lot to me per-
sonally--is that many of the people at the *Examiner* have the feeling that the interns should be
obligated to them.   That makes it into a paternal
thing, which is especially bad when it's a Black-
white thing.   There's a problem on both ends: a
feeling of obligation that we have that makes us
unable to break out of intern status as long as
we are there.   With Rufus and Cherise, the *Examiner* had to decide if they wanted people who
needed the program or people who needed the certificate, and they decided in favor of the person
who needed the certificate.

Supervision

The best thing would be to have a full-time supervisor. People that have just learned can teach it better because they know what to teach.

Trainee Reduction

I can't tell, because there were never four [when I was there], but what I found was that it helps to have other people, because you can really help each other. It's easier to criticize people your own age, and it's easier to take criticism. Other people say four wasn't workable, but I can't say.

Staff Attitude

There is the blatant racism of things like the article Greg's letter was based on, but most of the racism is the paternalistic kind, the more insidious kind. People thinking they can help minority people. They were mostly very well-intentioned people. They lose their Black people and they think it's because other places make better offers. If someone is a good writer and he's Black, he's a valued commodity, and the program should be for people who are not valued commodities. Most people who come from journalism school can't really report that well anyway, because they haven't been chasing stories.

Professional Training

The job I have now is so easy. The program didn't really train me for it, but working on a newspaper trains you for working on a paper. I'm going to be doing interviews and that I kind of learned at the *Examiner*. I learned how to write news stories. It was valuable for me, but it wasn't as valuable as it could have been. I respond where I have a large body of things to do and a defined structure. The problem is that you

can't criticize the program without criticizing
the paper, and the paper has a lot of faults. I
think it's a valid program, except it makes the
people at the *Examiner* think they're doing something and they're really doing as little as they
can get away with. There was a lot of pressure
so they did it, and since then they've been back-
tracking slowly. The thing about it is that the
program brings the only youth and vitality into
the paper that's there. I think it does more for
the paper than for the people that have been in
it. During the slack period between interns, when
Kieran was gone and Susan was in Berkeley and
Les was off somehwere, the newsroom was like a
morgue, and then the new interns came in and it
was lively and fun again.

GAIL (WELLS) CHRISTIAN, fourth week intern, interviewed at the *Examiner*, March 8, 1970:

Staff Attitude

The people that you work with are cool. You
wouldn't encounter any overt racism, but I have
on occasion read things in the paper or on the
editorial pages that were in my own humble opinion racist, but nothing you could put your
finger on. I think that all in all everybody's
nice and helpful. It's a work relationship and
I don't have political conversations with people
because I don't want to get involved.

Indoctrination Charge

I only do apolitical stuff and the only criticism
I ever hear is journalistic criticism. If there's
any indoctrination, I guess my turn hasn't come
yet.

Professional Training

I don't have anything to compare it with, but I
feel that by the time the program is over, I will
be a qualified reporter. In the journalism class
at night I learned a lot. I have nothing but good
things to say about Hugh Bernhard [teacher of the
class at that time]. The class should be compul-
sory before the trainee program so you can start
right off with a certain amount of knowledge.

Evaluation

I think the intern program is a really good program, but it's too new. I think the test of the
program is employment. What's the matter with all
these programs is that once you go through and
feel confidence, then either you can't find a job
or you find yourself underemployed.

Another interview with GAIL CHRISTIAN, at her home
in San Francisco, June 18, 1970:

Why did you quit the Examiner program?

To go to KQED and become a TV reporter. Television journalism is where the money is. All your
big newspapers are merging and, as this happens,
you have fewer people employed by newspapers and
more and more people looking for jobs in TV.
There seems to be more opportunity in television.
I don't know anything about the background of the
other applicants for KQED's program, but I would
say that because I could write a basic news story,
I think I had an advantage. I was in their program two months. I went from one apprentice program to another. KQED offered a little more money,
like $20 a week. Now I'm going to Columbia for
broadcast journalism, then I'll be working at NBC
in Los Angeles. Ford Foundation pays free room

and board and $37 a week while at Columbia; NBC
pays transportation and pays you your regular
salary while you're there.

Are all these programs serious attempts to bring
Blacks into the media or are they an attempt to
say, "Well now, don't say we're not doing anything because we have a program"? Most programs
aren't really minority oriented. They take someone already employed who makes a decent salary
and is just changing from one occupation to another. Into the media then will go a particular
kind of Black person, one who is able to function
without conflict among whites.

After about the sixth week, an intern can cover a
routine story alone, so they're getting the services of a reporter for $80 a week.

Black people are suspicious of Black professionals
anyway, without them going to work for what they
consider an anti-Black newspaper. They treat you
probably like they would any white reporter.
What you write is either going to be omitted or
watered down, anyway, if they tell you anything
they wouldn't ordinarily tell a white reporter.

It seems like a Black reporter has some sort of
responsibility to the Black community in what
they report and how things are reported. It's
also very difficult for a white reporter to get
the news--it's really very hard if it's a Black
story. We're going to have to do something.

ALONZO (LON)DANIELS, interviewed at his home in
San Francisco, February 3, 1971

Pay

I have it pretty easy; we don't pay much rent.
If I wasn't organized and didn't have other people I could depend on, I don't think I could have

made it. I couldn't live on $90 a week. I could
live, but I wouldn't offer my services to anyone
for $90 a week. I accepted the $90 a week because
they were giving me something that I wanted; I
wanted to acquire the skill.

It's rather hard for me to say whether they should
pay more, because they could get a guy in there
who just couldn't express himself in the manner
that they want: Maybe he couldn't adapt to that
style, and they would more or less just be stuck
with him. I do have some sympathy for them and
their problems. Thirteen weeks isn't a very long
time. If a guy knows what he's going there for,
I don't think $90 presents that much of a problem.

Assignments

On Saturdays, when there's not much work to do,
everybody does rewrites. I think I got stuck
with a lot of dirty work, but I think it was dirty
work from which I could learn something. Even
though it's boring, there's still a challenge to
write it in a readable way.

Supervision

Yeah, there was adequate supervision. They didn't
tell me what to do; they more or less told me how
to do it. They would come up with suggestions,
because I wasn't that great on ideas of what makes
good stories, but they would give me details of
what happened and then I could make out of that
story what I wanted. They would say, "Do you
have anything planned?" And I would say no; and
then Cline would say, "Do you want to come with
me?" He didn't start *telling* me what to do until
I got to know him real well, then he would say,
"Come on, Daniels; get off your ass and come with
me."

Trainee Reduction

I think they should cut it down to one at a time.
There are so many little tricks that you have to
learn, and even though there are two of them, they
very seldom tell you the same thing. Cline tells
you to look out for one thing, and Ludlow tells
you to look out for another.

Staff Attitude

In terms of specific incidents where I personally was treated unfairly because I was Black--I
wasn't aware of any. I felt that some of the
news and the way they play up news was very racist. That didn't hurt me individually, but it
hurt me collectively as a Black person. I was
hurt by some of the things in the paper.

Indoctrination Charge

They're trying to orient you toward functioning in the system as it exists. What they're
actually doing is they're showing you what it's
like. That has nothing to do with the writing
thing. And things aren't as rigid at the *Examiner*
as they must be other places in the system.

Professional Training

I do believe you should be an adequate reporter
after the program--not a good one, but an adequate
one--if you adapt to the style. I do think I
could get a job and do the work. I honestly got
what I hoped to get out of it. There may be de-
fects in the program for other people that are
looking for something else, but for me it served
the purpose. I will go on in writing. I do
plan to go on in journalism. What I would really
like to do is to try my hand at freelancing or working part time for a paper. If I can get an idea

that will sell, I don't think I'll have trouble
writing it. I feel I had the basic stuff when
I started. I just had to learn the technical
aspects of reporting. I think I had the writing
skill when I went there.

Evaluation

Just going out and asking questions of different
people, your knowledge of how the bureaucracy
works is increased. I don't think most people
ever find it out.

That's the beauty of the intern thing, that you
are getting turned on to how the system works.

It's made me more tolerant of reporters, but not
more tolerant of the Establishment. It's made me
less tolerant of the Establishment because I've
learned how deliberate it is. A lot of times
before, I would excuse people, saying that they
were ignorant, that they didn't know any better.
But I have come to the understanding that a lot
of people do know better.

LOUISE EUBANKS, interviewed at her home in Oakland,
February 9, 1970:

Recruitment

Lynn Ludlow called me personally. I had met him
at the college but I didn't really know him. This
was just something they had going primarily for
minorities and I was the only spade around. It
sounded like something worthwhile getting into.

Pay

It would have been nice to make more money, but
learning was more important than money. I didn't

need such a great salary. If you were self-
supporting, I suppose you would have to have
more. It's a trainee program.

Bylines

Many of the stories we went out to cover were on
deadline, so the reporter had to write those.
Also there were union stipulations: One of them
was that we couldn't take a major story from a
reporter. Most of the sections I went in I did
something that was published. Every time I wrote
something like a feature story, I got a byline.

Supervision

It wasn't like a school where you have a hired
teacher. Obviously they didn't have that kind of
close supervision. Some of the others needed
more supervision. But...it's hard to say. I
would say that for the group of trainees, and
we were the first, it was a reasonable system. I
think most of us learned a great deal and supervision was close. Maybe three reporters would
critique one story, which was confusing.

Trainee Reduction and Staff Attitude

I encountered various levels of prejudice, but
it didn't really bother me because that wasn't
what I was there for and I have encountered it
all my life. It would be very easy to make the
same comments Rufus did in his article in *Ball &
Chain*. But again, I'm over 30 and things don't
look the same. This is not to say I didn't see
all the things Rufus saw. I can understand
thoroughly what he's talking about and I felt in
many instances the same things, but at the same
time I met many beautiful people. I met some
groovy people and some weirdos. But as to the

reduction of trainees, I hate to see it, especially in view of the increasing need for Black journalists.

Staff Attitude

It's hard to categorize, but generally I'd say they were friendly, sincere. I had more than one reporter say to me, "You know, we newspaper people know that we've neglected the Black community and we don't really know how to cover the news." There was an open admittance to guilt. I didn't give a damn about their guilt; it means nothing if you don't change. I was there to learn something.

Indoctrination Charge

These men were teaching us the way they were taught. They weren't unkind. And this is the broader way that Rufus didn't say or explain. The training was valuable because it did teach you how to write a story in a certain way; therefore, it was not inadequate. But that every story should be written this way or that you should strive for this form always would then be inadequate. Life isn't an inverted pyramid much anymore, anyplace. Training is a kind of indoctrination anyway.

Professional Training

They helped me to develop the confidence to write for media print. Their faith in me helped a great deal. I know that I had not written enough there, but I know that I can do it now. I think the program was very helpful because it gave me something I could never have gotten in a school setting. It's an entirely different emotional involvement to meet a daily deadline. In a college newspaper you never really see the workings of a newspaper in the same way. You hand your copy in, and the next time you see it, it's in print. You really didn't see the editor sweating over it. That's very exciting. I think I would have had more difficulty in getting a job without the program because papers respect it. It's far more valuable than just a B.A. in journalism; it talks a lot louder. I have a greater chance now to get a job than my white counterpart.

Evaluation

The Kerner Report really racked up a lot of newspapers to tell it like it is. They want it but they can't use it yet because they haven't changed. Rufus wanted to tell it like it is, but they're not ready yet. They have to dispense with some of the old forms before they can accept a young Black reporter.

Jim Schermerhorn filled us in on a lot of philosophy; I learned an invaluable amount of philosophy of newspapers, and the reasons they do things, from him. He told us how he thought we should be trained, which was cool. And he encouraged me the most, on my novel.

They were terribly concerned that we didn't feel left out or didn't feel bored. Most always they were very concerned that they do the best for us. There were terribly boring and terribly exciting days.

I certainly hope that they will continue it and that more and more newspapers will start to hire minorities in some capacity involved in news reporting. But even more than just hire them as the only house nigger, the editors have to realize that they need a lot of policy change in their own hearts and heads about Black people. A Black

reporter knows, "I better not say this," or "I'm
not really free to discuss this aspect," because
he can feel the pressure upstairs.

Had I stayed on at the *Examiner* to work as a reporter,coming back and having them knock my stories, my report to you would be very different.
Being particularly a trainee and flitting about,
I didn't really get to the nitty gritty of it.
The pressure on a Black reporter is just tremen-
dous. It doesn't matter if they get a reporter
whose face is Black; he's not going to be grate-
ful to them for hiring him.

I had to cover a crime story with another reporter.
This young Black man had shot and killed a police
officer in Golden Gate Park. We were sent out
on the follow-up story the next morning. We went
to the young man's home, and as I remember, only
some young children were there. I think the thing
that angered me in that situation was that these
young people were untutored; they didn't realize
that they didn't have to open the door. It was an
invasion of privacy. I felt close to those ghetto
children and I resented it highly. The reporter
was very polite and beautifully nervous. I saw
these two things juxtaposed and it was an interesting experience. Someone told the child (on
the phone or something, I don't remember) to get
the reporters out of there, and he hightailed it
out. He had to come back with something--I
understand that--but he was nervous and that was
good.

Another time we had gone to Mission Emergency--
two reporters and me--to interview prisoners,
and the Tac Squad was all around. The reporters
told me: "Police don't like reporters, and after
Blacks they get hit first. So if things start,
just crawl under the nearest thing and stay there."

It was a little thing but it was important to me,
when someone takes the time to respond to you as
a human, to say, "You could get hurt."

The publishers were anxious to make it work. I
would prefer to give these men the benefit of the
doubt and say they were sincere. They seemed to
be involved with us. The program was a learning
experience. I'm glad I had it and, as the mother
of the group, I was determined to make it work.
They would tell me, "I am going to say things that
will hurt your feelings, and you are going to
have to tell me." That was important to me. Racism was there, but I'm moving on.

LANCE GILMER, interviewed at the *Examiner*, February
1, 1971:

Pay

If I had been single, it might have been adequate,
but even for a single person, it's not enough. It
was only $86 a week or something like that. I
had a $1,000 scholarship from a private source. I
was spending $30 a week more than I was making,
and that's like while eating hot dogs and ham-
burgers. I can't really blame them; I had a choice
about taking this.

Assignments

I wasn't trained. Even now I'm the highest paid
shorts writer in the country. I've been doing
shorts for so long, when there's a new editor on
the desk, he'll come by and say, "Write these 10
shorts." I tell him, "I'm a reporter now." But
I got to be well known for writing shorts and

they expect me to still do it. Copy boys do shorts. In fact, one copy boy was doing the baseball roundup while I was still doing shorts. He was getting trained and I wasn't.

Supervision

First let me praise two people: Glenn Schwartz-- there's a place in heaven for guys like him. He helped me a lot. And so did Dave Beardsley, when he had time. He explained to me what I was doing wrong. But other than that I had very little supervision, so I read 23 books. Burgin said I should read the sports page every day, so I did-- both the *Examiner* and *Chronicle*--so I was learning sports and technique from that. I got supervision from reading other people's work.

I think if I had been younger and not used to being by myself, I would have quit the program. The lack of supervision has hurt me and it's helped me. It hurt me because I'm very cynical about advice I'm given. I don't take their advice, because when I really needed it, I didn't get any. And it's hurt me because I'm alienated from the staff. It's not their fault, really. [In reducing the number of trainees,] I think they were finally getting honest that there were no jobs. Also, you can't train a person in 13 weeks, although if you spend a lot of time with them, maybe you can. But when a person comes into this program, he's being bull-jived, because you can't learn in 13 weeks. I think Lynn got smart about it. You don't offer people a piece of cake and then give them a piece of moldy bread. This is no reflection on Lynn or Al. And I don't know about cityside--they might spend a lot of time with the trainees on cityside.

Evaluation

The philosophy seems to be: "Keep them off the streets so they can't throw bricks." I think the program ought to be abolished or it ought to tell it like it is. If they tell you, "Hey, we got nothing for you," then I can see them going out and throwing bricks. If the *Examiner* were sincere they would have a bureau in the ghetto.

Fillers are nice when you start off, but I think you should assign somebody to the trainee. Jam into that 13 weeks four years of learning. At the end of 13 weeks you'd have somebody with some background.

I put myself in exile by moving to this desk in the corner. I came over here because I felt silly sitting on my hands while everybody else was working. The thing you need to learn is the mechanics. And even now I'm not sure of my mechanics. Every day I learn a little. It's taken me nine months to get where I am now. Maybe I think I should have been here after 13 weeks. One of the primary problems is the insecurity. The industry is getting smaller and smaller every day. I don't have 13 weeks of my life to waste. I want to do something for the Black people. Sports is dominated by the Black race; I can find out their story, what's bugging them; these should be brought out. The happy image is what we get; they never talk to Muhammed Ali. He's a beautiful individual, but they present him as a clown.

Rufus was upset because they wanted a hard-core Black and he was hard core. Like when I was working in Chicago, they said they wanted hard-core Blacks, so I hired hard core, and they said, "We don't want them--we want nice guys."

The pay is ridiculous, but you can't blame the *Examiner* for that, because you're told before you

start that you are going to receive peanuts. But
I don't think you would mind peanuts if you got
the tree of knowledge with it.

I've never seen a more patient people than the
Black race. The war ended in 1865 and we are
still paying a penalty, so I went from slave to
free slave. The only reason I'm sitting in this
room right now is because I'm Black. I don't even
know if I'm qualified.

CHERISE GREEN, interviewed at her home in Oakland,
July 1970:

Pay

I felt it was as fair as they could possibly be
without exploiting themselves. It's not as good
as the post office, but while you're training,
you're not supposed to get all that dough. You're
not earning it. I thought it was fair enough,
'cause those copy boys worked their asses off
sometimes and we were just hanging out a lot of
the time.

Professional Training

I went to press conferences, interviewed David
Halberstam (he wrote *The Last Odyssey* about Robert
Kennedy), and went to a breakfast interview of
Ricardo Montalban. I went to one conference on
ICBM missiles. The subject made me nervous. They
were using such doubletalk that I didn't know
what they were saying.

Supervision

It was a new thing--they probably handled everybody differently. I guess for me it was enough,

'cause I don't like to be bugged. I like to feel
it out for myself. Still, I felt left alone sometimes. I never had trouble finding someone to
answer questions; all my questions were answered.
Everybody was a great help. They were really cool.

Trainee Reduction

The more the merrier because with more we could
discuss among ourselves. We really got into some
thick things. With two you don't have much to
cling to. We had a blast and we got things down.

Staff Attitude

Sincere. And fair as they could be. Even on top
of the personal things, they seemed to go beyond
that; they seemed to really try to communicate.

Indoctrination Charge

No indoctrination. Me, I can't be indoctrinated,
'cause I tend to have my own opinion. The stories
I picked were what I wanted to write about and
sometimes it sort of shocked me that they let me.
There really wasn't that much heavy happening at
the time. If I had been really radical they might
have had to say something. Our thing was not to
revolutionize the *Examiner*. Rufus's was. Some
of the people he argued with have been brain-
washed, but you can't really turn a person around;
you leave them without a leg to stand on. I went
right from the *Ex* to the *Post*—I said, "Please
may I have two days off?" Then I got involved
with a theater group in San Francisco, so I cut
it back to half time. I stayed about one and a
half months—not very long—and of that, I worked
full time, maybe three weeks filing photographs.

Professional Training

More than adequate. They just didn't tell me
what I was going to be up against. They didn't
tell me it was going to be different than the
Ex. I was ready, as far as writing and reporting. Adequate for any newspaper. It was adequate just as long as the person wasn't expect-
ing it to be like the *Examiner.*

Evaluation

Just kind of opening a door and that's groovy
because a lot of Black kids never thought of
being a reporter.

Communications can get to be a problem, but when
you make an effort, you can break down all kinds
of barriers. It's Lynn's job and Alan's job,
and Rush's when he was there, and Jim Schermerhorn
sure helps a lot. There are a few that really
got involved and that were like our teachers.

I took the class at the same time as the program,
and it helped a lot. I'm an analytic person and
I have to get the moxie first. That class was
magnificent. Trainees should take the class
concurrently with the program. Some of them have,
I guess. I didn't really learn more in the class
than in the program; one sort of fed the other.
I could use what I learned in the class at work
and could use what I learned at work in the class.
I don't know which outweighed the other, but it
really helped, especially on sticky stuff like
in the travel department.

I wish I could have stayed on. I even asked them
could I be a copy boy, and they said no, it was
unprecedented. I really dig writing and some of
the people impressed me. They really got to me.

I don't have anything bad to say about it. They
were doing me a favor. It worked both ways, but
still, one doesn't concern the other. If it
hadn't been for the situation, an opportunity like
this would never have arisen. No other paper's
doing this.

———————

GREGORY GROSS, interviewed at the UC Berkeley campus, February 18, 1970:

Pay

I felt that because I was an intern, I didn't really mind not getting a full reporter's salary.
I didn't see any injustice in it. More would have
helped, though.

Supervision

Perhaps I had too much freedom. I made what I
considered to be a large mistake in trying to do
the best possible work that I could from the beginning. I was paid what was probably the ultimate compliment: I was turned loose. I was sent
alone to assignments sometimes. I felt honored
until I got out there. I would like to believe
that I came through it all right but every once
in a while I can still feel the scratch marks on
my neck.

I think one of the reasons I was turned loose
was not because I was that good a writer, but
because I seemed to be able to do the work all
right and the instructors didn't really have the
time they wanted to spend with us. They also
had their own responsibilities. I saw very little
of Lynn in the 13 weeks. The stories were cri-
tiqued by anybody in cityside whom I asked. I

didn't feel like I had to ask. If you asked for
help it was given very freely. You often got more
help than you asked for, which was always appreciated. On that particular point I was treated
very well. I owe my present writing style to
about half a dozen reporters at the *Examiner*. I
don't feel imposed on at all; I felt any advice
they gave was an improvement and to my benefit.
I went there with a knowledge of the pyramid style.
I didn't feel any hassle in that regard.

I think it would be a good idea if the people
responsible either had their loads lightened or
could devote their time exclusively to the interns.
Barron Muller on the police beat: If it were possible, he should be more involved. If he's not
a legend he should be; he's great. Helpful in
philosophy, method, making contacts, gathering and
sorting information, dumping it over the phone.
There are a lot of people around the *Examiner* who
do this very well. Jim Schermerhorn, he's a very
good judge and sharp critic of writing, in common
with Lynn. Russ Cone is a good investigative reporter; he makes you think. He knows how to ask
questions that make both the reporter and the in-
terviewee think. Mary Crawford is a phenomenon,
for general principles. I think Gale would like
to have more to do with the interns if he could,
but he has the responsibility of city editor. I
was very impressed with him as a person.

Trainee Reduction

If there wasn't enough supervision for two, I
can imagine what it was like for four. I don't
think four people would get supervision that
would really be adequate. Also it's a question
of desk space.

Staff Attitude

I don't think there was one particular attitude.
I encountered dislike from some, a great deal of
sincerity from others. I would say the sincere
ones were in the majority. By the fifth week it
seemed like I was just another reporter--no con-
descension. Very little racism. I suppose there
was some, nothing unexpected, since anywhere you
go where you encounter a great many whites--a
great many whites out of my age group--it's inevitable that you will encounter some racism.
But there wasn't a great deal, not enough to
make my stay miserable. Anywhere, you find what
you look for. I didn't go looking for racism or
indoctrination; I went looking for learning.
Those who went there seeking racism undoubtedly
found it. I don't think there are any red-necked
racists at the *Examiner*; if there are, they managed to keep themselves very secretive as long as
I was there.

Indoctrination Charge

Anybody who knows Rufus knows how difficult it is
to attempt to indoctrinate him. If there was
an attempt to indoctrinate me, it didn't succeed.
I think Rufus tends toward the editorial side of
writing, and you don't do much of that in cityside. It's not a matter of indoctrination; it's
a fact of life. Any editor with any sense of
ethics is going to raise up and scream. I think
there's a definite place for editorial writing,
but I don't think it can be all things to all
people in all sections of a newspaper. That
belongs somewhere other than in a news story.
Judgment and analysis, yes; opinion, no. And
only when that judgment and analysis are grounded
solidly on fact, not just for their own sake.

Professional Training

For anything except the New York *Times*, maybe.
Had the supervision been as constant as Lynn or
Al would have wished it to be, I think I would
be pretty well prepared for anything. As it is,
I am much farther along than I would have been
had I gone through four years of college in journalism. I came away feeling I had a four-year
education in 13 weeks. I think Black people,
journalists and non-journalists, benefit from
programs like this because whites have more access
to on-the-job training and experience. A program
such as this is totally unheard of where I come
from in New Orleans.

This is not a criticism, but something I could
point up with the case of Black interns: Many of
the Black interns who come there have a strong
desire to limit their writing to one specific
topic--Black people. The program is designed to
give a person grounding in general newswriting and
there's a basic conflict there. When a young
Black person is restricted from doing what he
wants to do, then the first thing he thinks of is
racism. I don't think that's the case.

It figures that when they go to work somewhere
else, they're not going to be able to specialize
in what they want all the time--everybody is not
going to be able to be a Black correspondent. Trying to specialize too fast is like trying to put
the cart before the horse.

RICHARD HARRIS, interviewed by telephone at his
home in Washington, D.C., March 2, 1970:

Professional Training

You could make out of the training program what
you wanted. Everybody had to write a feature story

and I wrote three of them. I worked in the sports department, too. I didn't get a chance to work on copy desk.

I think it's a meaningful program. The *Bee* has one but it doesn't amount to as much as the *Examiner's*. They kind of just throw you into the city room and say you are a trainee, but actually you are a cub reporter, and there's not as much guidance. At the *Examiner* they go over everything with you before you turn it in. At the *Bee* you go out by yourself, if at all. It's a sink-or-swim thing.

Supervision

I never had any trouble. When one of the guys wasn't around, the other one was, or you could walk up to the city editor and ask him a question, and if he couldn't help you at the time, he would ask someone else to answer your question. I needed a lot of supervision but if I didn't know what I was doing, I would just act like I did. I tried to keep busy at all times.

I wanted to make the program meaningful to me and figured the only way was to work myself to death. I learned more in that 13 weeks than in four years of college. Your college helps you, but there's no way possible it can give it to you in a professional way--writing under pressure and under noise.

Trainee Reduction

Maybe they are cutting back because of money situations or something. Four seemed to work then; I don't know what happened. By having just two, they can only work with them so much; some could need more supervision. I had already had

some experience writing. Maybe two would be better; I guess it depends on who you actually have
in the program.

Staff Attitude

No racism that I could detect. I wasn't even looking at it that way then. It might have been
there, I just really didn't look for it; I was
just trying to learn something. I liked the group
of people I was working with.

Job Placement

When I left they had gotten calls from New York
and Los Angeles asking about the trainees. I
graduated on a Friday and started working Monday.
I turned down jobs with AP and with Ampex. No
trouble getting a job. I had been working part
time at the *Bee* and when I left the *Examiner*,
Lynn called the *Bee*. They were trying to get in
contact with me.

Professional Training

Every paper has its own style, but once you get
the basic fundamentals, which I did at the *Examiner*, you're in. I had to learn the *Bee's* style.
I had style problems.

CHRISTOPHER KABUNGURA, interviewed at his home in
Berkeley, February 4, 1971:

Pay

For trainees, especially for Americans, I don't
think you can beat that. Of course, I'm talking
about young men who wish to get some training for
future years, like those residing with their

families. Lots of students are getting less than
that amount of money from their parents. But of
course it's not enough for me. I have a family
to support and I pay a lot of tuition for college.
Fortunately, I wasn't going to school at the time.
There are a lot of American students that are in
the same situation I'm in, but for young men or
girls who are being supported by their parents,
I think it's a good deal.

It's quite obvious that people would appreciate
more, but I don't think they're going to pay more
simply because people want them to pay more. Maybe they should really pay more, because after a
few weeks there, depending on your background, you
begin actually working, turning in some work just
like any other reporter, and as such I think they
should pay more.

Supervision

When I talk about supervision, I'm not talking
about someone standing there seeing that you do
your job, but just someone checking your stories.
And I think it was quite adequate. Actually, the
entire staff was so helpful that anyone could
have helped me. I asked many questions and many
people answered my questions.

Trainee Reduction

If they have the money, and I think they do, they
should train as many people as they can afford.
I'm sure there is enough help. The kind of help
these people need is not to have someone give them
instructions, but just to let them go out with a
reporter, write the stories, and then have the
reporter correct it. That would depend on how
many experienced reporters they have there, and
I think they have enough experienced ones.

Staff Attitude

I didn't get to know all of them, but those I knew
were among the best people I have met anywhere,
and I'm not saying this just because they gave me
the training. Those people are very kind and willing to help. I never had a quarrel all that time
I was there. They are jolly good people. I
didn't experience any racism, but usually people
tend to exhibit two faces. The *Examiner* has very
few Blacks.

Indoctrination Charge

Every newspaper has its own principles. If the
San Francisco *Examiner* wants to print things in
its own style, you can do two things: You can
put up with it, or you can go. You're not forced
to enter the program. They have their own style
of writing, but I don't see any mind trying to
indoctrinate the reporters to be conservative or
anything like that. Most reporters I have met
there are very liberal.

They can send you on assignments that would appear
conservative. They can avoid sending you to cover
something on the liberal side. For instance, if
there is a big Black Panther meeting, they may
send you to cover a John Birch Society meeting
instead. You go and cover that news and turn it
in as a piece of news, independent of your own
principles. I don't think that should affect your
own principles of thinking. I could write for
the *Examiner* and write for the Black Panther newspaper at the same time. So I don't see how they
can mess up your mind in terms of indoctrination.

Job Placement

They are helping me; they're giving me names to
call for interviews. The *Examiner* cannot promise

the trainee a job, they simply cannot. Training
them gives them a better chance of getting a job
and it's better than not having the training. I
can afford to work for a small newspaper because
sooner or later I'm going to return to Kenya. But
what about a Black reporter here who goes to work
for a small newspaper for $100 a week, less than
what a janitor makes? What about him? He's really in trouble.

I think the *Examiner* should have a really nice
understanding with other newspapers and let them
know what's going on in their program so the
chance of trainees getting jobs after they're finished would be really enhanced. In other words,
they should do just a little better to get their
trainees jobs. They should have more trainees.
It's better to hang around without a job and have
the training than to be just out there without
the training. With the training, something might
come along just like that. One more thing. They
have people stationed in Berkeley and maybe
Oakland. Since the *Examiner* covers some of the
Black ghettos, they should have trainees go on
those kinds of beats for a day or two. I think
they should have minority trainees go out in the
ghetto as much as possible. I don't know how they
can do it, but I think they should try to create
more jobs at the *Examiner*. They need more Blacks
at that newspaper.

CHRISTOPHER KNOWLES, interviewed at his home in
Berkeley, February 26, 1970:

Pay

I couldn't live on it. I don't think it's unfair;
I can dig it because of what they're doing. They
can't get money out of the government or the Ford

Foundation but they have got the best thing going
on the West Coast. That's pretty good. Somebody
ought to say so. It's not fair to say, "Should
the trainees get more money?" Nobody's giving the
Examiner money and it's costing money for them to
hang up their super people and it slows down their
machinery, and they don't get a return on it, really, because most people walk away. It's not the
the *Examiner's* place to play God. It's a money-
making business. That's for the government to do,
that's their business, that's what taxes are for.

The first or second day--second day, I guess--I
got appendicitis and went to the hospital for a
month. They paid me for the first whole week and
then a guy came around and laid some bread on us,
and they extended the program for me.

Assignments

The cityside is really out of sight at the *Examiner*--San Francisco is really the City and general
cityside reporters are really on top of what's
happening in San Francisco all the time. It's fun
to be able to do your thing and have it in the
paper. If you put a little too much of you in the
story and not enough straight news, it doesn't
get in.

Bylines

Most of the stories that I went out on were printed and then there was lots of stuff, mundane
things like rewrites and obits. You're low person on the totem pole so they throw that at you.
After you show them that you're paying attention
and know what's going on, they let you get out.
That's really fun. It's a nice school. I
couldn't get bylines on stories at the *Examiner*--
on photos, but not on stories.

I feel like, for what's going on, for what they're
doing, there should be nothing bad said right now.
Everybody's gotten into a habit of saying everything bad, but I don't want to see it turned off.

Supervision

It was enough for me, because I have done those
things for a long time. I've been hustling.
The only places I was, was where it's happening,
and that's fun. Another nice thing was that I
got to see what's really happening in San Francisco and I always wondered.

Trainee Reduction

Maybe they just couldn't afford it. Their money
people said, "Look, fellas, it's costing too much
bread." That's obviously what happened. At
least they have two now. Besides, the heat's off.
People are talking about ecology now, and they
don't have any more race problems.

All right, really, this is the product of Rufus
spending a page or two in the *Ball & Chain*, which
is some kind of jive name for a Black journalists' newspaper, and they spent most of that publication knocking the program. The *Examiner* has
responded by cutting it from four to two because
they didn't want to do it anyway. The only reason they did it was because they got some slick
reporters in there like Al and Lynn. They built
this idea over the bar and they swung it. Some
of the people made these bad noises and this is
what the *Examiner* has done. Sure. They can afford the program.

Staff Attitude

They were a groove. There were some people that
were put up-tight. The most cliquish of them
were the photographers, but because I'm a pretty
good photographer, they took it, and then they

got to be better. It's because they're artists,
they're different. They really aren't into a bag.
I didn't see as much racism at the *Examiner* as I
have at the *Mercury*.

Note added 2/28/71: Speaking of racism...[an ad-
ministrator] has said, "I am going to fire that
nigger." He made inquiries into my sex life and
has gone so far as to ask some guys, "Have you
been to Chris' house? How much dope is he taking?"
I have spoken to the union and my lawyer about
it.

Indoctrination Charge

Rufus is from Hunters Point. He talks a certain
way and uses a certain kind of semantics--they
say the same things but in different ways. I was
able to do what I wanted to do. I had one story
that I wrote better than the guy at the *Chronicle,*
who got a byline. I didn't.

Professional Training

I've been trying to get into the newspaper business for a long time, but you've got to go to
school. So I went to school for 13 weeks and I
got in. It's a way. Newspapers have a special
kind of format--journalese. One day I wanted to
go out and photograph some clouds. I know that
that's cool, but I have to hang that on something
or it isn't newsworthy. So I photographed clouds
and the weather plane coming in with the five
o'clock traffic and they ran it. Things like
that I wouldn't know how to do if I hadn't learned
the journalese of photography.

Evaluation

Overall I think the program has been super.
There's just one person who isn't working in the

medium, and that's Cherise, and she's off doing
her thing. As far as I know everyone is working
or in school in journalism.

It's better than anything I've ever heard about
as far as putting out successes. Cherise will
utilize it in her own way, like maybe someday
she'll write a song about newspapers. I think
the thing is a real success. There are lots of
things going on in there that could be better. I
couldn't get in that school now. They want people who are going to college now. This is a
certified society. If you aren't certified you
have to go out and work and get callouses on
your hands. I think they should run some more
people through there. They're doing a pretty
good job.

The greatest good for everybody concerned would
be for your whole report to be a plus thing. I
think they're losing by not getting people like
Rufus and me into that program, because I know
what's happening and so does he.

———————

JIM LEE, interviewed by telephone at his home in
Las Vegas, Nevada, February 27, 1970:

Assignments

No sports stories, all the beats were taken. The
Examiner is so big that most of the departments
there weren't aware of the fact that there was a
trainee program. Each time we were sent to a
different department we had to explain to the department head what it was all about. They were
friendly, but didn't know what they were supposed
to do with us.

Time Extension

The cycle before me they kept them all on for a month and two were still kept on after that. When our cycle rolled around there was no room for us. They explained it to us in the very beginning, so we all expected it. I looked around and called and talked to editors, and there was a place open in Walnut Creek. I had to move out of town anyway, and figured I might as well move out of the state.

Supervision

It kind of made it rough on the supervisor, because he would have to be doing his job plus training us. Lynn was about the best, I thought. If he puts in more hours, he should be paid more, or he should put in less hours on regular assignment. They're going to have to put the money somewhere. The difference between the *Examiner* and down here is that you work a lot more on smaller newspapers, simply because there are fewer reporters.

Job Placement

We had complete access to the phones, long distance, etc. I looked through *Editor and Publisher* and found the Las Vegas ad. It said they needed a news reporter with sports knowledge. Actually, it was a mistake; they needed two reporters, one for news and one for sports.

The thing is, I think since the whole thing is so rare, most small-town dailies will be very impressed with it. They would have hired me over the phone, but they had to have me down for an interview to make it look good. It turned out that the editor was trying to sell the job to me.

JIM LOGAN, interviewed at Stanislaus State College, Turlock, March 3, 1970:

Pay

I couldn't have supported myself. I lived with a friend and didn't have to pay rent. It wasn't a living wage, but it wasn't really discriminatory, considering that the reporters are more competent. Both the trainee and reporter are doing the same kind of work, but the reporter has to meet a deadline. There's a certain amount of pressure on the trainee--pressure to make the program succeed and to show them and to prove to myself that I had some journalistic ability. I don't think I succeeded. I'm glad the program was continued. They told us that it was mostly from what we did that they decided to continue. I was kind of surprised, but I was pleased about it.

Bylines

I don't think any [of my stories] were published; some of the handouts were. I wrote a story the last day I was there, and it was supposed to go in, but I kept looking in the paper and couldn't find it.

Supervision

I felt I needed more, but then I realized that under a newspaper production schedule they couldn't afford supervision. They would almost have to hire a man specifically to train us, or let Lynn free half a day. Lynn is pretty good, but there were some others that maybe could have done it, too.

Trainee Reduction

I kind of favor four people. I figure the more people you can expose to the business the better,

and get more Black journalists into journalism.
I have to sort of agree with them that two would
be easier to supervise than four, but on the aspect of exposure, I think as many people as can
be involved in the program should be.

Staff Attitude

There wasn't really any racism. I got some of
the identity bit, like, "I was brought up in a
ghetto, too." I didn't find many of them to be
too uncompromising or over-sincere. I think most
of them were fair about giving me help when I
asked for it, pointing out my errors without being overly critical.

Generally they said they were apprehensive about
approaching tight situations like the Panther
situation. Generally I am, too, because I feel
that the mere fact of reporting an incident isn't
enough, and sometimes contributes to an already
bad situation and causes a white backlash. Any
incident that the Black Panthers are involved in
is over-reacted to by a large portion of the citizens, who form their opinions from newspapers
they read. One paper, not the *Examiner*, reported
that the Black Panthers were respectful of the
cops because they were chanting, "Off the pigs."
He thought "off" meant "lay off."

I felt kind of guilty about taking the money I
was receiving. At one point I felt that I wasn't
improving enough. The program helped my writing
quite a bit, though.

Indoctrination Charge

There really is no set ghetto written language
and it would be difficult to follow. The same
word means different things to Blacks and whites.

It would require a massive revamping of journalism if it were to adapt to a certain language
culture that's not already in control. It sounds
like I've been indoctrinated pretty much. I
think if you are going to appeal to a large mass
of people, you can do this, but if you're going to
work on a metropolitan daily, you must adjust
to that style of writing. If you want to write
Black language you have to, I'm sorry, start
your own paper and go from there.

Job Placement

I haven't had any other work experience, mainly
because I've needed money to go to school and
there was more money working at the refinery in
Martinez than I could have gotten working at the
newspaper in my town. In effect, the *Examiner*
offered to help. They said if I was interested,
to look them up, keep in contact. Lynn said he
would continue looking around for things he knew
I was interested in, copy boy jobs or any other
programs. I feel like they will help me as much
as they can. I'm sure Lynn will, particularly.

Professional Training

I think it was due mainly to my poor background
from the beginning. I didn't have much writing
experience before that. I wasn't interested in
writing before my senior year in high school.
I had a teacher that learned I could write a
little and encouraged me. I think I need to do
a lot more on my own and try to learn. I'm not
properly equipped and don't have the tools. One
of my main problems was writing with enough so-
phistication: writing plain, simple sentences.
It's hard for me to collect my thoughts and type
it out within a certain period of time. That's
one of the reasons I'm not sure journalism is for
me.

Evaluation

I felt I wanted to do some more work, like I felt
it should have been longer, but I had to go back
to school. I had the feeling I wanted to come
back and try it again the following summer, even
though I was discouraged.

If they saw you sitting at your desk staring at
the walls or talking to your neighbor too long,
they would give you handouts to do. The moment
you finished one handout they would give you another, at times. I learned from them. At first
I thought they were kind of a bother because I
didn't see the reasoning behind it, but when I
found out it was to help me write more precisely,
I saw the reason behind it, and my handouts improved.

I thought it was a lucky break. The chance may
never come again.

———————

LESLIE McBEE, interviewed at the *Examiner*, March
6, 1970:

Pay

Sixty dollars a week isn't very much money, which
is what we cleared. But it was supposedly a training program, like going to school, and I had never been paid for going to school, so it didn't
bother me that much. But it's a relief now to be
on scale. I had supplemental income. There was
no way I could support myself on it.

Assignments

I don't feel like a spokesman for anyone. I
would hope not. That was one of the first things

I told Ludlow. It would be kind of limiting, and certainly I must have other qualities besides blackness. At the same time I was glad for the opportunity to cover Black stories, because in the hands of a white reporter there wouldn't have been the same treatment. My perspective was different.

Trainee Reduction

It's too bad more people can't benefit from the program, but I think two is really about all that they can handle. Four would be lost.

Staff Attitude

For the most part, I sort of like to say they meant well, but they never really quit treating you like an intern. There's a tendency to sort of mete out not very big stories.

Indoctrination Charge

I never really worried about brainwashing. I figure if you can brainwash me you must have a pretty strong position.

Professional Training

I'm not really sure about my reporting. I never really made the most of the situation. I'm just sort of dissatisfied. They did all they could toward teaching me the fundamentals. I would be more likely to recommend something like this as opposed to four years in college with a journalism major. You can't beat on-the-job training.

Evaluation

Generally speaking, the results of the program were beneficial. A lot of small things need to be worked out, particularly in the fields of supervising and evaluating the program on a week-to-week basis, evaluating what you have done. As far as reporting goes, I learned a lot because I knew nothing about it. I would recommend writing every day. You don't always have an opportunity to write every day, but even rewriting a while serves the purpose.

KIERAN MANJARREZ, interviewed at a coffee shop in Mill Valley, March 5, 1970:

Pay

I survived and as it was I didn't need anything those three months. If it were $20 more, there would be absolutely no complaint, because it's a trainee program.

I know that for myself, personally, I would have felt a bit more comfortable at $20 more per week. It's a tough job even as a trainee, and you're contributing after about the second week. Twenty dollars more would have endowed it with perhaps a slightly better sense of what our worth was. It's very easy to feel used, but only in moments of depression. When your pay goes up astronomically, you feel really great.

Staff Attitude

I know that there are people on that staff that are racists, but they kept their mouths shut. They're very few, one or two.

I *could* be a spokesman for the Mexican-American community, but there's a question of whether I would want to be. To be realistic, I would be a gadflyish type of spokesman. I would be reminding them about things just as much as I would be

reminding the Anglos about things. I could easily
be a spokesman for upper class or internationally
oriented Chicanos, because that's my background.
But to be a ghetto spokesman--no. I might know
the problems better than they do, but...

Indoctrination Charge

Anything in life is indoctrination. People run
one another, but man's a social animal, and that's
what it's all about. What Rufus meant--people are
throwing around terms that don't make sense--is
that there's a certain amount of indoctrination
that goes on in any society because there has to
be in order to have a community. Sure, the Establishment, whatever that is, has certain attitudes
and they have certain ways in which things are
done. The *Examiner* and *Chronicle* don't reflect
Black interests because the Black community is not
a community that has an interest lever to use.
This country is very much based on the uses of pow-
er. To that extent they're made to conform, but
that's in a much broader problem.

Professional Training

To have any experience at all counts for something
in the job market. I needed it for the actual
technical aspects, but whether I needed it as much
as anybody else, no. I needed to learn to write
under pressure and noise. I needed the acquaintanceship; in my case, it was an acquaintanceship
more than an apprenticeship.

Evaluation

I think it was a fascinating experience. I think
I grew with it to some degree and learned an awful
lot. I personally benefited most by dragging my
writing out of the academic corpse it was in. I
have learned to write a simple sentence. I can
think of criticisms of the paper and of why the

program exists, but not of the program. It was to get people interested and involved, and it did. I think it's doomed in its original intention of getting ghetto people involved. The paper doesn't have the obligation to make anyone a spokesman. It can't take somebody who can't write a sentence and teach them in 13 weeks to become a journalist. You have to take people who have a certain degree of proficiency in writing and talking and vocabulary--and a lot of things--and in most people these things come through schooling, though there are the natural geniuses. There might be some Chicano who is trying to write and trying to be a spokesman for his group and he's reached a dead end. That's the kind of person the program should help.

JEHANGIR PATEL, interviewed by telephone at his home in Hartford, Connecticut, February 26, 1970:

Pay

Journalism never pays well, but insofar as what journalists do get, I thought we were getting a fair shake. I could probably have lived on the $75 a week, but it wouldn't have been comfortable. I can live pretty cheaply when I have to, but it wouldn't have been much fun. More would be nice, but I don't think for anybody who takes a training program, salary should be any part of it. To some extent you want people who really want to learn; you don't want to entice them with pay, because then you get people who just want the money.

Supervision

We could always have used more. There's a question whether Lynn would be happy spending half

his time on the program. If you pull him out in
the morning, then you are hurting for deadline,
but in the afternoon, after the last deadline,
should be okay. But I don't think it should become one person's job exclusively. Everyone in
the newsroom should feel they are part of the program and should be willing to spend time, and
they did. I think the work should be more evenly
divided in that sense. But I think it was taxing
Lynn too much. He should be pulled off for the
afternoon, especially at the beginning, when you
need more supervision. Even if he wasn't working
training us, he could be looking around at the
job market.

Indoctrination Charge

If anything, they were indoctrinating us to be
fair and objective, if you can call that indoctrination. Now I'm on the labor beat and have to be
careful to be fair to both labor and management.

Evaluation

I thought the program was excellent. I told Al
and Lynn when I was leaving that I thought it was
a great program. I started working here in the
bureau and I thought that the program adequately
prepared me for that.

Most of the places that have training programs,
you are summer help and don't get any direction or
guidance. But we weren't really expected to write
anything; we were there to learn. We could have
been exposed to deadline pressure earlier. They
had us each write on minority problems. We spent
a lot of time on it and sort of questioned how
valuable it was. Finally, when they ran those
things, they sort of cut the hell out of them.

Even if they had asked us to pay to be in that
program, it still would have been a bargain. It
was better than school because you were learning
the real thing. I think they should have gotten
a lot more copy out of us than they did, and I
think maybe they should have spent a little more
time telling us about writing itself.

Almost my first day here on the Hartford *Times*,
they sent me to cover a story for the 250th anni-
versary of one of the towns around here and I
didn't know if I could handle it. But I managed,
and got a byline.

The bureau here was a lot more challenging than
the city staff there was; it's a lot easier to
get a story in San Francisco because there are
public relations people, etc. But here in Yankee
territory, you have to fight for your story; people don't want to talk to the press. I don't
know what they could do about that.

I don't need to remain anonymous, but please just
be sure to put in the good things I said about the
program as well as the criticisms.

DAVE RANDOLPH, interviewed at the *Chronicle*, March
1, 1970:

Bylines

I was given quite a few. What it boiled down to
was I didn't know a damn thing when I went in. I
thought I knew everything. They taught me a lot
of things that make for good pictures and were
extremely helpful.

Time Extension

I was a photographer. They wanted me to try some
writing during the program, but I didn't go for it.

I have trouble writing my own name. After my
initial 13-week training period, I stayed for an
additional eight weeks at first year scale as a
photographer. During those eight weeks I used
a company car and they sent me out on assignments
by myself.

Supervision

I got enough supervision when I needed it. There
were about four or five photographers there that I
couldn't have made it without. If they saw me
make a mistake, they would take me aside and tell
me how I could do a good job.

Trainee Reduction

Actually the three reporter trainees were a lot
to handle at one time, and I think that with the
limited number of people they have to work with
them, it's best that they have a smaller group.
I'm really disappointed, though, that they cut
out the photographer training.

They say they are looking for someone with great
potential, but if they went on that basis, I would
not have gotten in. For some reason I just think
they don't want to have any more photo trainees.
The scheduling is difficult. In cityside they can
give them handouts.

Staff Attitude

I couldn't say I really ran into any racism but at
times there was some hostility or tension in the
air. They have 18 photographers and I noticed
this in maybe two photographers. Actually, on the
whole, when I was there I think the majority of
the staff was a lot friendlier cityside than here
at the *Chronicle.* Here it's cliquish--not a race
problem, but how they treat people.

Indoctrination Charge

We did have some pretty heavy rap sessions on many subjects, but where I was I didn't feel I was being indoctrinated. But there was a completely different atmosphere in photo department than in cityside.

There's only so much they can do with a picture. They either have to run it or spike it; they can't make it appear in a different form.

Professional Training

When I came here I had no more business being here than if I were starting quarterback for the Green Bay Packers. I was not qualified to work here. If they had more time, I could have learned more, but...ninety percent of my time was with another photographer and they would tell me how to shoot it. You can't fix a picture--if you blow it, it's blown. You couldn't learn in 13 weeks. I've been here about a year now and am just beginning to feel comfortable going out on a job. When I go out on a job now I can imagine how it will be. The situation will be familiar, at least sometimes. But before, I would think, "It's the first time I've done this, and I don't have any ideas." You just don't have the background, and don't know all the cliché shots.

Evaluation

I went into the *Examiner* knowing nothing. I came out with the basics, and I came to the *Chronicle* and got the experience. If it weren't for the program, I wouldn't be here.

ORVILLE SPRINGS, fourth week intern, interviewed at the *Examiner*, March 8, 1970:

Pay

It's not enough to live on. I think trainees should be paid more, but it seems to be a neces- sary evil. I left Pan Am after two years and was bringing home $115 a week. I'm divorced and have a child to support. I'm sure I could qualify for welfare.

Supervision

It's a little frustrating at times because some- times you may be a little reluctant to interrupt them for something that seems minor. But even- tually all the problems are gotten out.

Staff Attitude

Possibly a little misguided liberalism. It's nothing intentional, just a lack of experience in dealing with minorities and knowing the sorts of things that might offend. Our sensitivities get very built up after a while.

Indoctrination Charge

Sometimes there is a question of ethics or deci- sions in matters of editorial policy even on the simple sort of stories. We receive a critique on a matter of grammar and we feel that it's a point of view. If they should choose to indoctrinate, they have a very good opportunity, but I don't feel that they are. I do find myself just sort of taking a new point of view. I find that my point of view is changing and I don't know if that's good or bad. You do tend to see the world in a different way. I don't know if that's indoctri- nation or just seeing things in a new light.

Professional Training

> I think there may be undue pressure in such a
> program which sort of comes from the fact that
> there's such an eagerness to succeed on the part
> of the trainee. You're sort of being evaluated
> according to some nice Negro who they knew be-
> fore that wrote so well. And you just wonder
> how nice he had to be.

Evaluation

> As an educational experience, I really think it's
> superb. It does open your eyes to so many other
> things that are going on and teaches you to re-
> spond and see things objectively. It gives you
> new eyes to see things. As far as the success in
> job placement, I have been a little concerned
> about that. I really want to go into journalism
> and couldn't have without the program. It just
> sort of has given me a new perspective on things
> and an opportunity.

HOLLIS WAGSTAFF, interviewed at the *Examiner*, February 25, 1970:

Assignments

> My first assignment was the building of a new fire
> station across the street from the *Examiner*. The
> second was kind of like baptism by fire: Glide
> Memorial Church for a conference on homosexuality.
> I had city hall beat. I really didn't like that.
> I didn't understand the rhetoric. The federal
> beat was difficult, even though I liked it. The
> language and terminology that they used was so
> over your head it would take a dictionary to under-
> stand them. I got a kick out of the Hall of Jus-
> tice, especially during the day in the summertime.

When the Gay 90's was closed [for nudity] on
Broadway, the two defendants had to come to the
Hall of Justice. And I covered the trial of
seven Communists. It was like my first experience in Chicago without being in Chicago. The
judge had a problem.

I worked basically here in the city and went on
three beats. I don't think I could have become a
cub reporter right after the program, probably
because my writing wasn't up to standards, but
also because I didn't have the credentials, the
degree.

Bylines

The 13 weeks that I was on the program, nothing I
did got in; probably because I wasn't up to par,
which was probably right. I hate to see my writing constrained.

Supervision

I had basically just two major reporters that were
over me. That was one thing that we never had to
worry about. Anybody and everybody was more than
willing to answer our questions. That was indeed
no problem.

Trainee Reduction

I wonder about the reason. It was formally announced that they had cut it down. But to this
day I don't know why. Maybe two are easier to
work with. They needed the program, and they
liked the program. Maybe it's because of expenses,
but I doubt it. The first thing that popped to
my mind was that they couldn't afford it, but I
had to rule that out, because it didn't make sense,
but there was no telling why it happened.

Staff Attitude

You naturally have a few incidents, but I can't really think of any now. When you become a subordinate staff member, a copy boy, you become a faceless nonentity. When I was on the program, because it was a kind of pilot affair, everybody was as sincere as could be. Once you become a part of the "family" (and put that in quotes), then they take it for granted that you are supposed to know what you are doing. That's when you really find out the few little bad spots. What you thought was just somebody's bad day, you find out this person's days are all bad.

Indoctrination Charge

The reason why...[the environment] bothered me a little bit, and it still does, is that to have us on this paper was an emergency measure. Now, it's fine to have had Rush [Greenlee] run on "Black news," but that didn't change the whole structure of the paper. We won't change the structure because the reporter has no say so on policy. Rush couldn't stand to see his stuff tampered with.

The conflict comes when your view and their view don't correspond. To an extent I would agree with Rufus. You are indoctrinated to the American view and world view as seen by the eyes of the mass media.

I admire Rufus because he dropped out of high school and he could still out-write me.

Professional Training

Depending on your background, depending on what you knew before, you could probably work as a reporter after you got off the *Examiner* program. I don't think I could do it after three months.

It depends on how well developed you are, but
from my own standpoint, I don't think I could do
it.

I think that if the man has that degree, I don't
think he should have to go through a training
program. The degree should speak for him. To
train a person is to say, like, you are unskilled.
For us that's fine; we were unskilled and naturally had to be trained to perform. In that respect I could understand it. But for me to go for
eight years of college and then come back to this
paper and go through the training program--wow.
All you need to do is just tell me certain style
things that are different--fine--I'll catch on.

Evaluation

[It taught me to be] able to write and type and
just be able to communicate with people and ask
intelligent questions; the laws of journalism:
no libel, no slander. Everybody here is eager to
teach you. It's kind of a mother-father complex
away from home.

I didn't like news releases all that much, but
things that I did write, funerals and trials,
were very interesting. It went fine for me,
which is why I stayed on here, because I liked
the people. I feel different now because of the
position I'm in and because of what I have learned
since the program. You get to really know the
people you work with when you are on the receiving end. There are people that are very petty--
this you can overlook. And there are people that
are very nice. Depending on your awareness
level, the petty ones and ones you can't get along
with are a part of determining your world view.
You may disagree like hell but you see the world
through them.

Partial Index to Interns' Responses in the Interviews

Bailey, Gilbert E. and Paul S. Thayer
California's Disappearing Coast: A Legislative Challenge.   99p   1971
$3.00

Coons, John E. and Stephen D. Sugarman
Family Choice in Education: A Model State System for Vouchers.   118p
1971 $2.50

Greenfield, Margaret
Meeting the Costs of Health Care: The Bay Area Experience and the National Issues.   182p   1972 $4.50

Hawley, Willis D.
Blacks and Metropolitan Governance: The Stakes of Reform.   34p   1972
$1.50

Nash, A. E. Keir, Dean E. Mann and Phil G. Olsen
Oil Pollution and the Public Interest: A Study of the Santa Barbara Oil Spill.
157p   1972 $3.75

Nathan, Harriet, ed.
America's Public Lands: Politics, Economics and Administration. Conference on the Public Land Law Review Commission Report, December 1970.
395p   1972 $7.00

Rivers, William L. and David M. Rubin
A Region's Press: Anatomy of Newspapers in the San Francisco Bay Area.
(F. K. Lane Series)   172p   1971 $5.75 clothbound, $4.50 paperbound

Scott, Mel
The States and the Arts: The California Arts Commission and the Emerging Federal-State Partnership.   129p   1971 $3.00

Scott, Stanley, ed.
The San Francisco Bay Area: Its Problems and Future. Franklin K. Lane
Volume III.   499p   1972 $8.00 paperbound, $11.00 clothbound

Scott, Stanley and Harriet Nathan, eds.
Adapting Government to Regional Needs: Report of the Conference on Bay Area Regional Organization, April 18, 1970.   306p   1971 $5.50

Smith, R. Stafford
Local Income Taxes: Economic Effects and Equity.   220p   1972 $4.50

Tompkins, Dorothy C.
Local Public Schools: How to Pay for Them? Public Policy Bibliographies:
2.   102p   1972 $3.50
The Prison and the Prisoner. Public Policy Bibliographies: 1.   156p   1972
$4.00

Books may be ordered from The Institute of Governmental Studies,
109 Moses Hall, University of California, Berkeley, CA   94720

(Prepayment requested for orders under $5.00. California residents add 5 percent sales tax; residents of Alameda, Contra Costa and San Francisco counties add 5½ percent sales tax.)